OPTIMISM IN THE VIRAL PANDEMIC

Our New Normal

Romain U. DuFour, III

ISBN 978-1-63885-285-8 (Paperback)
ISBN 978-1-63885-286-5 (Digital)

Copyright © 2021 Romain U. DuFour, III
All rights reserved
First Edition

Covenant Books, Inc.
11661 Hwy 707
Murrells Inlet, SC 29576
www.covenantbooks.com

CONTENTS

CHAPTER 1

COVID-19 Can Be Overcome

In March of 2020, life as we know suddenly became different. This was the first time that many in America heard of the COVID-19 virus. It was initially thought that the virus only affected a particular group of people, which was the elderly.

As time has progressed, this invisible virus has changed the world in a plethora of ways. One way that this worldwide pandemic has altered the lives of many is by affecting the ability of millions of people to have sustainable employment. Due to the threat of this highly contagious disease, a high number of businesses in this country have been forced to shut down.

A second way that this pandemic has influenced the world and society is through isolation. For example, isolation from others is the recommendation by various doctors and infectious disease experts who are studying this phenomenon. Millions of people are confined inside of their homes in order to maintain control of this mysterious foe.

There are many who are frustrated with how our world and society has become. No longer can an individual come and go as one pleases. Some Americans are not permitted by certain countries to travel or visit due to the virus spiraling out of control in the United States.

The mental health of many of the citizens of America has become an enormous problem. With the uncertainty of the society and world in which we live, there are many who do not have anything to anticipate or look forward to. When you factor in the fact that isolation is strongly encouraged, it is understandable why many are succumbing to anxiety and depression.

Not only are the threats of unemployment, isolation, anxiety, and depression—issues that have the potential to become a reality in many of our lives—dealing with the threat of contracting the COVID-19 virus can also complicate matters. Sadly, some are experiencing some, if not all, of the issues that are plaguing our world as a result of this perilous illness. This virus has many not knowing what to do, or how to act.

One's attitude and mindset is extremely crucial. If you do not have a positive mentality, then there is an increasing chance that you will have a negative response when life becomes more challenging. COVID-19 is a virus that has affected every individual in our society in some capacity.

We all have either one of two reactions in regard to this virus. One reaction that I do not recommend for any individual living with or affected by this disease is fear. Fear can cause or accelerate a negative outcome.

The other reaction that one should have is positive acceptance. I am not in any way stating that one should jump for joy in the midst of a life-threatening viral pandemic because that reaction is unrealistic. My suggestion for all living in and through this epidemic is to try to remain positive as well as composed.

I hope that no one experiences this terrible virus. Realistically, this worldwide epidemic does not have any favorites or partiality. Anyone can become infected with this illness, and this is why this illness is so alarming.

There are highly intelligent experts with familiarity on infectious diseases that are suggesting to the public to follow certain protocols in regard to COVID-19. From the genesis of this pandemic, experts stressed to all individuals that they should not touch their eyes, nose, or mouth after coming in contact with others or surfaces that were touched in public. Also, experts said that everyone must wash their hands with soap and water for at least twenty seconds to decrease one's chances of becoming stricken with the virus.

After a while, it was determined that it was not just the washing of hands that became vital to lessening the spread of the virus, but masks and physical distancing were also suggested in taking the necessary precautions in combating COVID-19. There have been some who refuse to listen or take heed to the precautionary measures in which many of the experts have recommended. I believe that this virus can be overcome when the individuals in each community do not become defiant, but follow the recommended safety measures and guidelines that are established.

When a community and a society are working together as a whole, there is not anything that these individuals cannot overcome. The United States can overcome the spread of COVID-19 by citizens holding themselves, as well as their neighbors, accountable. At this present time, it is mandatory that all individuals, from toddler age and older, comply with wearing a mask in public.

Quarantining for at least ten to fourteen days when exposed to the virus has helped in previous months. In the middle part of spring to the early summer of 2020 was a time that this country seemed as though it had the disease under control. When the United States took a more proactive approach in combating the spread of COVID-19, statistics showed that there were fewer fatalities.

I am aware that it is difficult to get every individual on board with self-quarantining and isolation because as humans, we are naturally social beings. The National Basketball Association (NBA) seemed to provide the blueprint on how the COVID-19 virus can be prevented. All of the media, as well as the basketball players who were playing meaningful games in a confined arena and space commonly referred to as "the bubble," were subjected to mask wearing, daily tests, quarantining, and isolation from the outside world.

To my knowledge, I did not read or hear of one case of someone in that environment becoming stricken with the virus. If the NBA can have that kind of positive outcome, then this country as a whole could also overcome the spread of this pestilence. For those who are less fortunate and cannot afford a face covering, there are some local government officials and volunteers who have supplied masks in various community drives for free. If our nation can adopt an aggressive approach to combating this serious disease, this pandemic could be defeated.

This virus will test how mentally stable one is. It is understandable how one can become pessimistic about the times in which we live. Although we are living in unprecedented times due to the outbreak of this unforeseen pandemic, I would like to offer you a challenge.

My challenge to everyone living during these challenging and chaotic times is to never lose hope. I believe that hope is always the spark that everyone needs. There is a phrase that my mother would say to me when I was a boy, and that phrase is, "It will not always be like this."

In my opinion, this phrase has always been a reference of hope for me. When a reliable vaccine for treatment is available to the masses in the near or distant future, an individual must never relinquish one's hope. I am cognizant of how easy it is to throw up one's hands in disgust, especially when everywhere you turn, there is constant reminders of this pestilence.

So what happens if you, unfortunately, test positive for COVID-19? My suggestion is that you do not allow the diagnosis to take every ounce of your positive expectation that you have acquired in life. Sure, it is never pleasant to experience any type of sickness, but I firmly believe that having a high level of hope in the midst of a negative situation or circumstance can make a difference in how one approaches unfavorable events in one's life.

I believe that many people in the world have lost hope that they can experience sunny days in the era of COVID-19. For a majority of individuals, positive hopes and expectations decreased when the economy plummeted. Some do not realize how being able to live another day on earth is a chance for hope for tomorrow.

Do not allow this virus to deflate the hope that you can get better after becoming infected with the virus. Though the number of people infected with the illness is increasing, there are also many who were able to combat and defeat the disease. In my opinion, I do not think that those who have been fortunate enough to overcome the illness ever gave up hope in envisioning themselves regaining their health again.

Having a reliable support system will always influence an individual to not become defeated by challenges and trials. Support from others can result in hope for an individual who happens to contract the virus. Hope can become infectious when those closest to you have a positive mental mindset.

Now we are in a world and society in which a hopeful outlook on life is greatly needed. Those who share a mindset of hope are in the minority. As long as one has the right mind, that individual should be feeding it with hope.

One must be cognizant of the fact that we are what we have formulated in our minds and thoughts. If one is internally hopeful, then it can influence one's external well-being. In the era of COVID-19, do all that you can to keep your hope consistent.

Faith is extremely essential in every area of our lives. In regard to the COVID-19 virus, faith can help an individual develop a spiritual outlook and perspective. With genuine faith in the Almighty, an individual who happens to contract the virus can develop the faith and courage to combat the illness.

No one, not even a man or woman of faith, can say for certain how one will react to being stricken with the COVID-19 virus. Sometimes negative events and situations could help an individual develop perseverance. Perseverance is a vital factor in overcoming anything difficult in life that we will encounter.

The COVID-19 pandemic has changed life vastly and dramatically. Because of the severity and seriousness of this pestilence, one must rely upon someone other than oneself. Our Creator and Lord and Savior should be our top priorities in these difficult times.

Although, personally I have remained hopeful and optimistic despite what is occurring in the world and environment around me, I would not have a high level of optimism if it were not for my faith in the Most High. Instead of listening to the gloom and doom of local and national news, I suggest that one strives for spiritual guidance during this pandemic.

Having a relationship with God is really what matters in a turbulent crisis, such as COVID-19. No one can face this virus in one's own strength. This is why it is imperative that the individual encountering the challenge of COVID-19 has some semblance of faith.

Relying upon one's faith is the wisest thing that an individual can do. Without an adequate amount of faith during any negative and difficult time in life, an individual will not have the antidote to overcome. Hopefully, if one did not have enough faith initially, that individual will obtain it after a successful recovery from a life-threatening disease epidemic.

Realistically, this virus could consume the most positive and upbeat individual. The COVID-19 virus does not discriminate between an individual who is God-fearing, or the individual who is incorrigibly wicked. While this pandemic continues to spread, strive to do all you can to have a positive mentality.

Though life is currently uncertain, one must live one's life in a joyous way. Take time to enjoy conversations with friends and loved ones, whether it is by phone or face time. Encourage your neighbors and loved ones to have faith while remaining cautiously optimistic.

The reason why I suggest that one remain cautiously optimistic is because of the unpredictability of life. It is humanly impossible to not have a day without some type of challenge or issue, even if it is minimal. A goal that all living in the COVID-19 era should focus on is physical and mental stability.

Maintaining unshakable faith during a highly contagious viral outbreak can be accomplished. One can never have undeniable faith without exercising it. This virus is the perfect opportunity to overcome the disease by hope and faith.

My hope for all individuals is that no one becomes afflicted with this perilous virus. Unfortunately, the way that it looks, there will be a plethora of people who will suffer from the illness until there is a dependable vaccine. The COVID-19 virus has been a thorn in the side for many.

There is not anyone walking on this earth that would welcome a serious illness or disease in one's life. In fact, many would rather avoid falling ill at all costs. Some view sickness as a sign of weakness.

Sickness and illnesses are a big part of everyday life. Most ailments could become avoided with lifestyle changes. For instance, diabetes can be avoided if one becomes cognizant that one cannot eat unhealthy foods as well as living an active lifestyle, which includes exercising.

In regard to the COVID-19 virus, it is not as simple to control like other illnesses and diseases that can be prevented. This particular pestilence is worldwide. It is not confined to a specific area or particular part of a country.

As I am writing this book, it has been revealed how this particular virus, COVID-19, is airborne. Many of us have to go outside to either work or carry out various chores and tasks. The worst thing that anyone can do during this uncertain time is, develop a mindset that they will eventually become infected with COVID-19.

Dr. Norman Vincent Peale, the late great minister and author in the twentieth century of the *New York Times*' best seller book entitled, *The Power of Positive Thinking*, coined the phrase, "Law of attraction." In the law of attraction, it really does matter how one thinks. For example, if you think internally when you wake up in the morning that you will not have a pleasant day, chances are that your entire day will also not go well.

With the COVID-19 virus, one must not allow becoming infected with the illness to have dominion over one's mind. If one is constantly thinking internally that one will be among the millions of people who are affected by this pandemic, then there is a great chance because of the law of attraction, it could happen. This is an example of Dr. Peale's poignant phrase.

We all have a specific type of energy that we give off to others. There are only two types of energy in which each individual gives. One's energy is either positive or negative.

Now I am not saying that if your energy is always positive that you will not experience negative situations or occurrences. Sometimes bad things happen to good-and-positive people. This is just the way of this fallen world.

What happens if one is a positive person who happens to become affected with COVID-19? I believe that the positive individual will not focus on the fact that they are stricken with the illness. The individual with a positive outlook will have their mindset on how they can recover.

For some, the road to recovery from the virus has become a bit of a challenge. COVID-19 affects various people in varying ways. If you happen to become infected with the virus, how are you going to respond?

What type of individual are you typically? Do you respond to challenges in life by complaining, or do you accept it and learn from them? In regard to COVID-19, the only thing that one can do is develop acceptance. An individual afflicted with the virus does not have any other alternative.

This virus has been the determining factor in regard to one's mental grit. Becoming stricken with COVID-19 is not easy to endure. There are a plethora of side effects that is a result of this virus.

One side effect is pain in the chest. Another physical effect from this virus is shortness of breath. If an individual can overcome those symptoms, then that individual should have a more positive outlook in regard to life's challenges.

I am aware that it is difficult to become optimistic while experiencing the life-threatening symptoms of COVID-19. This is why it is imperative that the individual experiencing the virus have an optimistic vision of their recovery. Overcoming any type of illness or sickness will definitely influence the individual to have a positive perspective.

There have been instances in which an individual afflicted with the virus have found a new lease on life. Some are fortunate enough to have a second chance after coming down with the virus. When an individual values life, more likely that individual will exude positive thoughts.

In all my years, I have yet to see an individual overcome anything in life with a negative attitude and mindset. COVID-19 could realistically and potentially become fatal. A negative attitude of disgust can be just as detrimental.

COVID-19 does not have to be encountered with fright and negativity. Sure, the statistics of people affected with the virus, as of today, does not look promising, but those who become infected with it have a greater chance of defeating the illness now as opposed to when the outbreak initially commenced. Although, it is still upsetting to learn about one's COVID-19 diagnosis; many experts and doctors in the midst of this pandemic are becoming more knowledgeable in the treatment of it.

I must admit that the COVID-19 virus, though invisible, is extremely potent and powerful. As humans, we have the tendency to become discouraged by the unknown and also by what we do not understand. We must never yield to confusion and fear because those mindsets defeat a positive one. Instead, trust and have faith that you can conquer whatever challenges and difficulties life throws out at you.

The COVID-19 virus, although it is an infectious disease, is a challenge and trial in our lives that can be overcome in spite of the bleak outlook. We must continue to persevere regardless of the circumstances. All individuals living in this unprecedented era must rely on their resiliency and tenacity in order to overcome this viral battle.

We do not know what tomorrow will bring. This is why an individual must take each day as it comes. The COVID-19 virus should not stop anyone from experiencing joy.

As mere humans, we cannot control all that will occur in our lives. The pandemic that everyone is experiencing will have an individual lose his or her mind, and sense of self, if one allows it to. Every individual should do all that they can to avoid becoming afflicted with the virus, but living in fear of being plagued with the illness must not have precedence in one's life.

I can recall growing up in the 1980s. During the mid-to-latter part of the decade, there was also an unknown disease that was invoking fear in the United States, as well as worldwide. The disease which I am referring to is commonly known as the Human Immunodeficiency Virus or HIV. There were many who were perishing from this mysterious unknown illness.

Growing up during that time in our society, I can recall how anxious and worried many had become. When a plethora of individuals cannot grasp the root or origin of why many are perishing and succumbing to an unrecognizable illness, then most likely a fearful frenzy will occur. Sometimes living in fear will hinder one's ability to enjoy life or have a positive mindset.

Eventually, doctors and experts discovered how the spread of HIV materialized. During the peak of the HIV epidemic, many thought that it was a disease which only affected homosexual men. Soon it was revealed that heterosexual men and women were also becoming infected with this deadly disease.

After some time had elapsed, the cause of HIV, the virus that causes AIDS (Acquired Immune Deficiency Syndrome), became known. I must say that after experiencing the HIV/AIDS era and this current viral disease, there are similarities between the two infectious diseases, because HIV was also feared and life-changing like the present-day COVID-19 virus. Once people were aware of how the HIV virus is potentially transmitted through sex and by the spread of needles used to inject drugs, many commenced to take precautions by changing or altering their promiscuous lifestyle.

It was also later determined that HIV, the virus that causes AIDS, was easily preventable. An individual who was abstinent from sex and not a partaker in the sharing of needles for drug usage was highly unlikely to become infected with HIV. Though it is a disease that no one should strive to acquire, due to the research and knowledge acquired on the subject of HIV and AIDS over the past twenty-plus years, the fear of perishing from it has literally subsided because of effective treatment and drugs.

Although HIV is still an undesirable illness to contract, many who unfortunately suffer from the disease have hope. Today the disease has become extremely treatable. No longer are individuals fearful of perishing from the illness like they once were thirty to forty years ago.

COVID-19 is now the virus that is striking fear among many in the same way that HIV and AIDS once did. What is so alarming about the COVID-19 virus is that it is spread by minimal contact. One must realize that if one does not fear, then one has already taken the initial step in overcoming COVID-19.

Chaos and turmoil have recently become the new normal in our society. It seems as though with each passing day, there is an increase in regard to this perilous viral challenge. Sadly, due to this viral pandemic, many of us cannot enjoy the outdoors in the same way that we once did.

The COVID-19 virus has essentially forced many to become familiar with their homes. With the state of our world and society, the safest place for each individual is indoors. I am aware that being indoors is not ideal, but because of the uncertainty of this virus, I believe that this is the best-case scenario.

Previously, I discussed how the HIV/AIDS virus has been able to become less prevalent after an enormous outbreak. When the HIV virus was extremely widespread, I can recall how many, during that time, lost hope that there would be any viable drug(s) on the market which could alleviate symptoms of the virus or significantly prolong the infected individual's life.

Hopefully, in regard to one becoming infected with the COVID-19 virus, an individual could one day also have a potent drug or vaccine that can instantly help the individual infected have the assurance of overcoming the virus by not perishing from it. Right now, at this present moment, it might seem like this viral outbreak will never become defeated. As I previously mentioned, never lose hope that relief from this virus can come.

It will require a plethora of learning and patience from the experts as well as the public. In the meantime, do not allow pessimism and hopelessness to control your mind and thoughts. While this viral pestilence is dangerous and unpredictable, the courageous-and-positive individual will continue to press on in spite of what is occurring in our world and environment.

Personally, I cannot predict how the world will fare in the COVID-19 battle in the distant future. The information that we presently have now to combat the virus is better than not having any procedures and guidelines to follow at all. Though this viral outbreak is somewhat foreign, the good news is, we know more about this pestilence today than we knew in the previous months.

In my opinion, an individual becomes victorious over the COVID-19 virus when he or she is infected with it and can live to tell about it. Diseases and viruses of the past have fortunately been able to become controlled and contained. Although there is currently not a certified cure for COVID-19, the positive take from the prevention of the spread of the virus is that there are examples of overcoming a disease epidemic with containment.

Every individual in this country and worldwide has a model or example of a life-threatening illness becoming less of a factor in society. HIV and AIDS are not viewed in the same negative perception as it was in the beginning of that epidemic. Hopefully, COVID-19 will also one day be perceived as a treatable disease that is more likely to result in prolonged health instead of endless death.

Inner peace is something that many of us would like to have. In the era of COVID-19, peace is difficult for some to sustain. This is why it is imperative to have an outlet in these turbulent times.

One cannot and will not overcome this virus without having the mental and spiritual peace from within. Now is the time to seek it. While the world and society is in the midst of turmoil in regard to this invisible foe, you can avoid the temptation to worry by doing activities and things that will fill you with joy and peace.

When this perilous outbreak initially occurred in the state of Washington in early 2020, I knew initially that this pestilence would become a difference maker. For me, it did not matter how the virus originated; when this invisible disease spread in all fifty U.S. states, internally I had to make the decision, in my mind, about whether or not I would allow a pandemic to take me out of my inward comfort.

Do not get me wrong, what I have learned most about COVID-19 is that one must cherish one's life and health. As of now, no one can confidently say for certain that they are immune from contracting the virus. Some have followed all the mandates and guidelines in regard to the prevention of the illness and still unfortunately became a victim of the pestilence.

Another lesson I have learned from this epidemic is that an individual can take all the precautions in the world, but if it is in the cards for one to come down with this mysterious virus, in many instances, there is not much that one can do except attack the disease with courage and strength. If you happen to become infected with COVID-19, do everything in your power to not think about a negative outcome. Instead, think of the day when you will have a negative test result, stating that you do not have the illness.

Essentially, one must develop the peace from within, in accepting whatever circumstance that acquiring this virus might bring. I am not in any way being pessimistic because at the rate that this outbreak is affecting millions of people worldwide, there is a realistic chance that if you do not become stricken with the disease, someone close to you might become the one affected by it. COVID-19 does not have to cause one to abandon one's optimistic view of life.

I am aware that sickness has a way of affecting and destroying someone mentally as well as physically. In regard to the COVID-19 virus, yes, it could affect someone physically; but it is up to the individual who is infected with the virus to not allow it to have its way on an individual's positive mentality. Mental strength can only derive from an optimistic and hopeful mindset.

It is difficult to have any type of positive outlook while in the midst of headaches, shortness of breath, or chest and muscle pains. My hope for the individual experiencing these symptoms is that they have the positive vision of having their pain diminished. Overcoming COVID-19 will require the stricken individual to rely upon one's patience and positive mental imagery.

Briefly, I discussed how it is imperative that an individual rely upon one's faith, especially if one unfortunately becomes infected with COVID-19. I have seen instances in which an individual suffering from this virus has rededicated one's life to God. Hopefully an individual who is affected by this pestilence, whether he or she has recovered from it, or a close friend or relative who has fortunately combated the illness is thankful for a happy and positive outcome.

With all that is occurring in the world, we need to have an authentic relationship with the Creator. I believe that an individual who has a spiritual mentality will be able to experience inner peace and strength in spite of unfavorable situations and circumstances. COVID-19 can challenge the most spiritual and religious individual, but only a relationship with God can help an individual deal with the challenges pertaining to this viral disease epidemic.

No one can fully prepare for the COVID-19 virus, but trusting in the Creator can make a significant impact in how one is able to have positive thoughts despite of a life-threatening illness. Trusting that God has full control over all of life's challenges and circumstances can influence the individual to strive to overcome the illness while also becoming more accepting of this mysterious invisible threat. In regard to the Word of God, an individual who is a daily reader of it understands that challenges and trials are used by God to help one grow spiritually as well as build godly character.

When an individual is able to overcome the COVID-19 virus, it is ultimately because it is the will of God. He (God) gives the doctors the wisdom to be able to help the individual who is suffering from the virus, the ability to recover and overcome it. If an individual happens to contract the pestilence, hopefully that individual gives the Creator the credit for overcoming and becoming victorious over a life-altering virus.

This virus is an ongoing battle. There are some who have battled the illness for several months. Some suggest that the individual who becomes infected with this infectious disease will never be the same individual they once were.

It might be true that the stricken individual may not be able to live their life in the way that they did pre-COVID-19, but when you examine it from a positive perspective, the individual who is able to recover still has precious life. I can recall how some who have experienced severe symptoms of the illness initially thought that they would perish from it. When these particular individuals were able to survive great pain and distress, I am certain that the individual developed a positive mindset, as well as hope.

COVID-19 is overcome with a team effort. First the doctors and medical staff working with the stricken patient must be committed to the infected individual's overall recovery. Secondly, the affected individual must listen to the instructions and advice of the medical team. Lastly, the COVID-19 patient must have faith and trust that they will recover and overcome COVID-19.

CHAPTER 2

When All Else Fails, Rely on Optimism

The COVID-19 virus is a test of an individual's internal optimism. Due to the fear of someone contracting the illness, there are many who do not have any hope for the coming future. With the chaos and turmoil in our society, as well as the threat of becoming plagued with the virus, it is difficult to remain positive.

In regard to one becoming pessimistic due to the COVID-19 virus and all of the other issues in our world and nation, I would suggest that one strive to find something in life to be optimistic about. Personally, my optimism has never wavered since the onset of this pandemic. The reason why I can remain positive and optimistic is because I always reflect on how the Creator has brought me out of all the situations and trials I have experienced in life.

Now I am uncertain about how this worldwide epidemic will play out. I do not know if it will ultimately become a thing of the past, or if it will be here on earth wreaking havoc until the end of the age. This virus will have an individual questioning whether or not life will return to the way it was before this global viral outbreak.

I do not think realistically that life as we once knew will be the way that it was previously. As members of this world and society, we must learn to have the ability to adapt. Our world is constantly evolving and changing, and there is not anything that you or I can do about it.

Sometimes it is difficult to accept change. Those who are optimistic in life have the ability to embrace whatever comes their way in life. An optimistic individual is not naïve or ignorant of the challenges that lie ahead in our world, but these particular individuals make a conscious choice to not allow what is going on externally to have a negative effect on them.

Firmly, I believe that an optimistic attitude in the midst of chaos and turmoil can become contagious. If one person chooses to remain optimistic in limited interaction with others, it can also have a positive effect on the next person. When this occurs, a community as a whole can have an optimistic mindset.

It requires enormous effort to remain optimistic when life is increasingly becoming difficult to bear. This is the time to develop an optimistic outlook from within. No one can control the future events that will occur.

One thing that we all can control is our thoughts and perceptions. When it comes to this current pestilence, which the world is experiencing, one's perception of it really does matter. If one perceives it from a fearful perspective, one's ability to have an optimistic mindset becomes nonexistent.

Because of the negative outlook stemming from the virus, it is imperative that we all hold on to the optimism that we do have. While listening to various news outlets that report on how this pandemic is negatively affecting our world and nation, I can understand how one could become consumed with negative thoughts. One must not allow the potential of becoming stricken with this virus to influence one to become a full-blown pessimist.

Optimistically, my hope is that this country, as well as the world, will be able to deal with the chaos and fear from this virus. It saddens me that children and young adults are currently unable to enjoy their education experience. Due to this pandemic, those who are students are limited in various school activities.

There are some who are in school who are unable to attend high school and college basketball and football games because of the limited capacity of fans allowed at these sporting events due to this widespread epidemic. Although there are limitations for fans that want to attend games, several months ago it seemed as though live viewing of games would be in danger of not happening. The optimist in me is thankful that at least there is some form of entertainment and escape from the negative news of this viral pestilence.

It is a good thing that there are still sports and entertainment that the average individual can still enjoy. When the pandemic initially came into existence, it not only affected the lives of everyday Americans, but also the wealthy athletes and entertainers in this nation and worldwide could not perform for the masses due to the nationwide shut down of many of our countries. I can recall viewing old games and movies, which was the result of the sports and entertainment industries having work stoppages.

Will there be better days ahead in regard to the containment of the COVID-19 virus? I hope so. Our world and nation cannot sink any lower. This nation as a whole is in need of an optimistic boost.

For the past several years, there has been a downward trend in optimism for many in our world. When you factor in a major infectious disease epidemic, there is a cause and reason why so many are headed in a negative direction. There is little that one can do to battle anything negative when one's optimism is gone.

There are a few things that one can do to boost one's optimism even in the midst of a deadly pandemic. First of all, I suggest that an individual pray and meditate daily. Secondly, the individual should only talk on the phone or FaceTime with those individuals who bring hope and optimism into their regular conversations. Lastly, if you find yourself yielding to negative thoughts due to the COVID-19 virus, be encouraged that if you happen to become infected with the virus, you can survive it.

The mind is powerful, and that is why it is imperative that you feed it with positive and uplifting things. One cannot feed the mind with hope and optimism by dwelling on how severe this viral outbreak has gotten. You only have one mind, and because it is sensitive, it is imperative that one avoids feeding it with negative stimuli.

Viewing and watching news on the subject of COVID-19 can become overwhelming. If you can, keep the negative news to a minimum. One might not be cognizant about how continuous coverage of the COVID-19 pandemic is detrimental to an individual's heart and mind. When the negativity is minimized, then optimism can blossom.

It seems as though COVID-19 is having its way among the nation and the world. I believe that this particular virus is threatening the optimism of many individuals. As someone living in the era of COVID-19, my hope is for all to envision a time that the pestilence will not be prevalent in our world and society.

I understand that there is a possibility that a viable vaccine for the epidemic might not work, or cause an allergic reaction. Right now, everything in regard to a vaccine is up in the air. Although there is uncertainty when it comes to this perilous virus, we all have to live life the best way that we know how.

When difficulties come into your life, you must not allow the challenge to steal your joy and optimism. Sure, the reality is that there is an invisible viral threat that does not care about one's position in society, or where one resides. This virus affects the wealthy, as well as the less fortunate.

What can one do in the midst of a dangerous pandemic? The only thing that I suggest is that you live your life one day at a time. Living one's life day-to-day can minimize negativity and fear of the unknown. There is not anything that one can do in regard to this pestilence except take the necessary steps to protect oneself or the members of one's family from becoming another COVID-19 statistic.

An individual in this era of COVID-19 must not live in fear and paranoia. One's mindset should be focused on one's dreams and goals. I understand that some aspirations must be put on hold due to these unfortunate circumstances.

If the dreams and goals that you set cannot be accomplished during this difficult and unprecedented time, then try to set new aspirations. There is a certain optimism that dreams can bring to someone. My suggestion to the individual with goals in this unpredictable era of COVID-19 is to try not to set them aside if you can.

In my opinion, having goals and dreams could become a positive distraction. Now I do not believe realistically that these aspirations will erase the fact that we are living in a horrible pandemic in one's mind, but achieving these goals can raise an individual's level of optimism. It is always wise to constantly set goals and aspirations for oneself regardless of what is happening in the world.

No matter how dreadful life becomes as a result of COVID-19, strive to anticipate a brighter day. Before this infectious disease commenced to affect many, I can confidently state that I experienced some good days, as well as not-so-good ones. There is always something that happens in life that always has the potential to affect and threaten one's joy and optimism.

The COVID-19 virus has reduced the optimistic attitudes and mindsets of the masses. It has single-handedly turned many into prolonged pessimists. One must continue to hold on to the hope of one's dreams and aspirations, which can brighten one's life if and when it is accomplished.

Suffering is inevitable in our fallen world. Due to the onset of COVID-19, there are millions worldwide who suffered from this infectious disease. I am cognizant of the fact that many have suffered unfairly from this outbreak.

No one enjoys experiencing the pain of an illness or disease. If you happen to experience any type of discomfort, it is easy to not have hope and optimism. For some, pain and discomfort is a way of life.

My mother has rheumatoid arthritis. She has experienced pain throughout her entire body for years. There are some days that the pain in her back, knees, and joints are more severe than other days.

What can she do when the pain is continuous? Just like I previously discussed, an individual must strive to live the best life that they can, even in the midst of pain and discomfort. This does not mean that the individual with pain should abandon one's optimistic attitude on life. If you live long enough, there will always be some type of ailment or illness that will affect your life in one way or another.

Individuals who might be experiencing the effects of the COVID-19 virus must not get down on life. I am aware of how there are some individuals who lived illness-free lives before the spread of the virus. These particular individuals do not know what it is like to experience sickness and pain.

When an individual is accustomed to a life void of pain, it could become difficult to accept one's current circumstances. I can only imagine how an individual must feel when they are suddenly stricken with an illness after years of relatively good health. The individual might not know how to deal with suddenly having an illness and being among the sickly.

This is why it is imperative that each individual living in this COVID-19 virus era develop the realistic mindset that anyone can come down with any illness or sickness in life. It does not have to be the COVID-19 virus exclusively that an individual could experience; there are also other types of illnesses that could affect anyone at any time. An individual who is suddenly plagued with a pestilence such as COVID-19 should immediately focus on one's treatment.

If an individual who is affected by the COVID-19 virus is fortunate enough to live through it with some residuals of pain, then that individual is still thriving. This pandemic is responsible for killing a plethora of individuals in this country, as well as worldwide. Combating and surviving a major infectious disease outbreak should result in an individual becoming totally optimistic.

Though this virus can overwhelm you, be cognizant of the fact that suffering will not always last. Spiritually speaking, sickness and disease will soon become a thing of the past in the near future. One has to hold on to the hope that the temporary pain, in which one might be presently experiencing, will soon become a nonfactor one day. Suffering will not always last but optimism can.

Our world and society is facing a crisis in COVID-19 that has challenged everyone from young to old. Sadly, no one, including newborn babies, is immune to becoming infected with the virus. Because experts on the infectious disease are scrambling, as I write this book, on how to solve reducing the effects of this invisible destructor, it is considered a great feat if an individual can survive the illness.

I have personally seen through the news media some unlikely people who recovered from the virus, as well as some who one would think would survive being infected with the virus, due to their physical prowess, that did not. It is definitely out of the ordinary when a baby can survive and recover from COVID-19 and a world-class gifted athlete does not. This infectious disease is quite baffling when you think about it.

Surviving COVID-19 is extremely difficult. The individual who unfortunately is infected with the virus does not have the luxury of family and friends supporting them in the flesh. This is obviously not by choice, but the process of not allowing others to be in the hospital room with an infected patient has been recommended by doctors and experts since the beginning of this worldwide pandemic.

It is difficult to remain optimistic and hopeful when one is battling the disease in isolation. An individual infected with COVID-19 essentially has his or her self and the doctors and nurses who are caring for them. Hopefully, the medical staff that is caring for the COVID-19 patient is full of optimism and positive vibes.

If an individual can survive being stricken with the COVID-19 virus, there is not any other medical challenge that the individual cannot also face. One has to have a strong-and-positive mindset in order to endure this debilitating illness. Due to the isolation that this virus causes, optimism is strongly needed.

The doctors and the medical staff of the COVID-19 patient must have empathy as well as a bedside manner. It is because of a loving and compassionate medical staff that a victim of this perilous virus has an inkling of a chance of developing optimism in spite of an unfavorable prognosis. In regard to the long road of recovery from COVID-19, an optimistic mindset will become a key factor in overcoming the disease.

For the friends, family, and loved ones of those who happen to suffer from this unpredictable invisible pestilence, I would suggest that you do not lose hope that your friend or loved one can recover and survive the illness. Sometimes in life, a situation or circumstance could seem rather bleak, then all of a sudden an unexpected positive outcome commences to manifest. There is always hope and optimism that any dire situation can eventually turn in a positive direction.

An individual who is battling COVID-19 from home or a hospital bed must rely upon those times in one's life, in which one was able to overcome a trial. I believe that the Creator can get anyone through a no-win situation. One must do their part and not allow the battle of COVID-19 to diminish any positive hope for one's future.

Chances are that many living in the COVID-19 era do not have any hope and optimism in the days that lie ahead. There are events and situations in our world and society that do not offer any individual a chance to have a positive attitude. As I observe many individuals living at this current time, it is revealed in their posture and body language that, for them, all hope is lost.

I have come to the realization that life must be lived as optimistic as possible. The best example I can think of in regard to living a life full of optimism while experiencing great agony is when little children are enduring other life-threatening illnesses and challenges. These brave young children innocently put smiles on their faces in spite of the pain they endure.

Just like those precious boys and girls who naturally have optimistic thoughts, I suggest that adults battling the illness also adapt that childlike optimism. The goal for anyone in life is to live the next day better than the previous one. An individual without optimism could essentially become a detriment to oneself.

The individual experiencing COVID-19 should not think that their life is over because they just happen to become infected with a perilous virus. When an individual has that mindset, they are essentially surrendering to the virus. No one can honestly say that they will react to receiving the news of testing positive for COVID-19 positively.

There are some who choose to allow the virus to have a negative effect on one's psyche. These individuals have already said in their mind that this virus will take over. Let's be clear: I will be the first to tell you that I am no expert on the COVID-19 virus.

I am aware that this illness can have its way with the most fit and optimistic individual. Individuals who are severely ill due to the COVID-19 virus, I am not conversing about. The individuals with whom I am referring to are the survivors, the ones who were fortunate enough to be blessed to win their battle.

Seeing individuals complain in a pessimistic attitude and tone after surviving a life-threatening disease bothers me. An individual with that mindset is oblivious to how ungrateful bickering and complaining from the effects of a perilous infectious disease is viewed by others. It should not become a burden for those who love the survivor of COVID-19 to care and nurse the stricken individual back to health.

Some who have been affected by COVID-19 are not the same individual who they once were. These individuals might have painful reminders of the virus but still have the optimism and hope that they can one day return to the individual they were before their diagnosis. I am a firm believer that the mind can affect anyone in either a negative or positive way.

In regard to an individual having optimism, it is a mindset and attitude for the victorious. Surviving and having life is definitely a cause for celebration and optimism. Although an individual is on the mend after experiencing COVID-19, that individual should never relinquish their optimism and hope in overcoming this particular adversity.

When it comes to having optimism in the era of COVID-19, it can become difficult to sustain. There are increasing numbers of Americans perishing each day. Also, the virus has forced many to alter their daily regimen and routine.

Some are receptive to change, while others are not. If change is required in order for one to remain alive, then it should be welcomed. From an optimistic perspective, altering one's daily habits and routines could benefit the individual in the long run.

Since March of 2020, the workplace environment has become quite different due to this infectious virus. Many are able to work from home. In addition, children and their parents also have the option from many school districts across the country to learn at home virtually.

While working from home and having one's children also learning from the friendly confines of one's abode, I can optimistically see how it could be viewed in a positive sense. For example, the parent who is fortunate enough to be working from home will not have to deal with the daily grind of reporting to work at a specific time. Secondly, a single-parent who has a child also remaining at home does not have to be concerned about their children's whereabouts or childcare. Also, parents do not have to arrange for their child to be picked up from either school or daycare.

I understand how, initially, having one's child or children at home can be overwhelming and frustrating. The optimist in me would also bring to the attention of the stay-at-home parent(s) that they are more void of worry at home as opposed to having anxiety from having their children attend school in person. Due to the unpredictability of this virus, no one can always initially detect who is a carrier of this mysterious pestilence.

Although I am not a parent, I would honestly be less optimistic in sending my child to school because of the potential of the lad contracting the virus from another classmate. Thus far, studies have shown that children are not as prone to perish from COVID-19 as adults. Though, children can also die from the effects of the virus, and some experts on infectious diseases claim that children can also become carriers of the illness.

Presently, there are some children who are returning to school in some states in America, and some parents are concerned. Earlier I mentioned how one can obtain optimism in the midst of a pandemic although the parent and child are at home. On the contrary, I could also understand how a parent and child could become optimistic in resuming their normal routine of going to work and attending school.

One reason why I believe that a parent can become cautiously optimistic in returning to work is because of social interaction. Due to the onset of this pandemic, many in the workforce have had limited interaction with coworkers. Another reason for optimism for the individual who is returning to work on a limited basis, is lack of boredom. Unfortunately, it can become extremely boring for the parent, as well as the child, to only have one another as their only interaction. As human beings, we tend to respond positively in the mind and body with optimism when we can engage socially.

We must not lose hope and optimism that the COVID-19 virus can become tamed. This country has a plethora of competent doctors and experts who are working feverishly for a remedy to combat the disease. Because the United States typically leads the way in medicine, one's optimism should not be replaced with skepticism.

Though I am cognizant of the struggles that many have encountered due to this pandemic, I have also seen, throughout this ordeal, those who have responded to the negative circumstance with resilience. In order for an individual to demonstrate resiliency, that individual must have a certain amount of optimism and hope. The United States, as well as other nations worldwide, has endured a plethora of catastrophic events recently.

COVID-19 has definitely caused nations that were at odds with other nations to not dwell on their differences. Some nations are doing better in the battle with COVID-19 than others. America, thus far, is considered one of the nations which has not fared well in regard to the containment of this viral outbreak.

There is always hope and optimism that the tide will turn on the right side of this epidemic. Patience and hope will help in the quest for a viable vaccine. As a nation, we should ask ourselves, "Why not become the nation to lead in the development of a reliable vaccine?" Scientists and experts must also not lose optimism and faith that the spread of COVID-19 can be resolved.

Overcoming this infectious pestilence is what everyone living during these uncertain times should be focused on. It does not do any good to point the blame at the country or nation in which this virus might have originated from. As a country and nation, we are in the midst of this pandemic together.

During these unprecedented times, do not abandon the power of prayer. It is through prayer that optimism comes into fruition. If you have not commenced to pray, I suggest that you, the reader, start now. You might say that the prayers of a single individual are invalid and will not make any difference.

When many individuals are genuinely and sincerely invested in the welfare of others by praying, an optimistic effect can and will develop. As this occurs, instead of the spread of a perilous virus, prayers and optimism will defeat and overcome it.

I believe that optimism in the midst of a negative circumstance, like the COVID-19 virus, cannot be attained without an active prayer life. It is never too late to begin and end each day in fervent prayer. Instead of focusing on the astronomical death rate, one should strive to become engaged with the here and now.

Imagine how wonderful it will be in a world void of COVID-19. My hope for all who are affected by this virus, which includes you and I, is that you do not allow this pandemic to steal your optimism and zeal for life. There is always hope for a positive outcome from utter chaos.

Without an optimistic attitude, an individual will lack positive energy. There are many who have allowed this pandemic to drain them physically, spiritually, and mentally. From the time that an individual wakes up in the morning until it is time to retire to bed, there is continuous coverage on COVID-19.

Hearing upsetting-and-negative news daily will have an effect on an individual's level of optimism. When it comes to whether or not one will allow this virus to deflate one's positive vibe, it is essentially up to the discretion of that particular individual. It is heartbreaking to me when I see many living in this unprecedented era succumb to having negative energy or a negative mindset.

If you consider yourself a religious or spiritual person, then you can rely upon the Creator to fill you with positive energy and optimism. In my opinion, it is useless to get caught up on how it was in the good old days. As individuals and members of society, we must move forward.

Is this viral pandemic inconvenient? I would not be telling the truth if I said that this virus is a walk in the park. Sure, we are living in a world and society in which we must constantly take daily precautions. Doing minute activities within a day, such as shopping for groceries and getting a regular checkup at the doctor's office, is considerably different nowadays.

As a society, we must not challenge the taking of precautions from our local businesses. I optimistically believe when everyone complies to what some experts are requesting, which is the wearing of a facial mask or covering, the sooner the spread of this virus will dwindle. An individual who is noncompliant in regard to suggestions and orders from state and federal government on the subject of wearing a protective covering are essentially being negative and difficult.

The COVID-19 virus is a widespread trial and hardship. This hardship has affected many in various ways. I cannot comment on how difficult it must be to have to support a family while not being able to have a reliable and steady job due to this pandemic.

To the man or woman struggling with the issue of steady employment and survival, I would say to you, "Do not allow your situation or circumstance to keep you in a pessimistic mood or mindset." Because of this pandemic, many families are in a difficult bind. An individual who is economically and financially affected by this unforeseen occurrence must hold on to a positive and optimistic mindset that the Creator can make a way out of no way.

It is essential to the morale of one's family that the individual(s) heading the family continue to exhibit optimism in spite of lack. I am cognizant of the fact that an individual's optimism alone cannot pay the bills. What can come from an optimistic attitude and mindset is positive energy. As humans, we tend to feed off of the energy of another individual. One's positive energy can be the difference between landing a necessary job or interview, or losing out on that opportunity.

Each day is always a blessing, whether one unfortunately becomes infected with the COVID-19 virus or not. This pestilence will overwhelm the individual who does not already have an optimistic view on life. An individual with a realistic and optimistic perspective on trials and challenges in life will always battle them with optimism and hope.

As the days of living with COVID-19 is progressing, one's optimistic attitude is needed now more than ever. The battle over this viral outbreak is won when society is able to experience a positive outcome. We cannot have the outcome that many desire without having the needed optimism required to eventually overcome the disease.

Currently, there is a dreary feeling in the air. A decision must be made in regard to an individual yielding to dread. Some are oblivious to the fact that we have more options in life instead of succumbing to pessimism and hopelessness.

In these past several years, I have seen many who are down on life. When you add COVID-19 to the mix, there is an understandable cause for stress. For some, there is not any reason to be optimistic.

The world in which we live has been on the decline before this viral pandemic. Morally, the righteous values that many in our country once had has decreased. If one does not practice integrity, then typically that individual will have a negative outlook on the world as well as life's challenges.

This explains why COVID-19 has destroyed the positive perspective of many. Some have taken advantage of victims of the virus by running false scams. One would think that these criminal acts might decrease due to the severity of this outbreak.

If one continues to allow the decline of our society to affect one's optimism, then those who practice evil and wickedness have won. The COVID-19 virus is also an invisible wicked foe. It has suddenly turned many individuals' laughter into deep sorrow.

Do not allow this epidemic to turn your optimism and laughter into sadness and pain. One has to find it within oneself to take a moment to appreciate being alive. With all that is occurring in this world, it is definitely a cause for optimism when an individual can see another sunrise on the horizon.

Thus far, we as a society have been living in a cloud of hopelessness and despair as a result of this viral pandemic. I challenge many of you reading this book to change the narrative. You can alter your mind and body with an optimistic and hopeful attitude and outlook.

We all must rely upon optimism because pessimism and negativity will get us nowhere. In the COVID-19 era, a healthy mind and body can elude many. A pessimistic attitude is just as damaging to the overall wellness of an individual as this virus.

COVID-19 may or may not enter your body. If it does not affect you physically, it can still have a negative effect on your mind. The battle and war over this virus is either won or lost when optimism is at the forefront.

CHAPTER 3

Do Not Obsess over It

Since the onset of this pandemic, news of this potentially deadly virus has flooded the airways. Every television station known to man is mentioning the COVID-19 virus. Our world and nation is in a dangerous reality.

As a nation, it is understandable why the pandemic is a continuous topic of discussion. I can recall how some of the experts initially downplayed the peril of the virus. Also, they said that there was not any cause for worry.

In the weeks after the statement was made that the virus was "essentially harmless" and "an illness that only affected the elderly," things commenced to change. All of a sudden, the spread of this viral outbreak was not only prevalent among senior citizens, but the young and the healthy would also have a reason to become filled with anxiety and discomfort. COVID-19 soon became a viral pandemic that would affect people of all ages and ethnicities.

Most humans would like to think that they have control over their lives. This virus has demonstrated that this is not the case. Some are so panicked by the potential of perishing from this virus it has now turned into a natural obsession.

Being obsessed with anything in life is never a good sign. When an individual is continuously thinking about something morning, noon, and, night, it can manifest itself into a full-blown psychotic break. Once this occurs, the mind and body becomes negatively affected.

I believe that many individuals are not alone in their obsession over this pandemic. Personally speaking, it is extremely understandable how one could become deeply invested in hearing about this infectious disease. It seems as though there is not any break or relief in the discussion of the epidemic, especially in the mainstream media.

Frankly, we live in a culture and society in which sensationalism is emphasized. In this country in particular, it does not require much for many to become infatuated with someone or something. When a media outlet has a story that can affect the masses and influence a plethora of people in either a positive or negative way, an obsession could formulate.

COVID-19 is not just some other story. It is a viral pandemic as well as a highly contagious infectious disease. There are many facets of our society which have been altered due to the spread of this invisible threat.

Life, unfortunately, will not currently resume to normalcy. Because of this heartbreaking reality, many are in a panicked state. Those who are in that state will typically obsess over the problem or issue that is the root cause of that particular reason for panic.

We all must take some time to escape what is discussed on television, as well as on social media. Though there is some good in which one can experience from being informed, too much information on a negative events or circumstances will essentially cause the individual to become obsessed over something we currently cannot control, which includes the COVID-19 virus.

Due to the shutdown of many businesses around our country in the mid-months of 2020, every individual has experienced the effects of this pandemic. Small businesses, such as barbershops and hair salons, were enormously affected. Since many were either working at home or staying there, many have not seen any need to keep up with their physical appearance.

Some might suggest that there is not any need for personal grooming because many are forced to remain indoors. One might say that they do not have anyone at home in which they have the need to impress. I beg to differ that one does not have any other person to keep up one's appearance for.

The person whom one should impress is you. Just because these set of circumstances have become difficult to bear does not mean that one should let oneself go physically. An individual who continues to groom oneself the best way that they know how can still like the person who is looking back at them.

It is imperative that we all continue to carry out daily activities, such as exercising and grooming. Studies have consistently shown that exercising helps with an individual's mood. In this era of COVID-19, having a clear mind and consistent mood is needed in these times of chaos and uncertainty.

Also, exercising and grooming can help an individual have something to anticipate or look forward to. I am cognizant that it is difficult to perform normal activities while a life-threatening viral pandemic is wreaking havoc in the world. Doing activities like exercising and daily grooming will help the individual with normalcy and stability in one's life.

In my own life, I have been able to avoid becoming obsessed with the threat of COVID-19 because I have not ceased doing the daily activities in which I enjoy. Each day, I anticipate daily grooming because it helps me to maintain my sense of self. My mindset in regard to performing daily activities is, I might as well continue taking care of myself because the COVID-19 virus itself cannot.

There are many who are giving their power to this virus. The reason why I am stating that the COVID-19 virus has dominion over many in this world and nation is because of the abandonment and neglect that the virus causes. Because of the fear and obsession which this epidemic has imposed, daily activities have been difficult to perform.

One must strive to have self-care in spite of the obsession over this pandemic. It will not make the situation in which we all are experiencing any better when one chooses to give this virus precedence in one's life. Choosing to enjoy each day in spite of obsessing over what could happen should be desired.

My suggestion to all who are living in this unprecedented era is to strive to perform the same activities that you did before COVID-19 became widespread, such as grooming and exercising, if you can. In my opinion, it requires great strength and courage to not allow this pandemic to turn daily tasks into an undesired chore. Obsessing and altering one's life due to the COVID-19 virus demonstrates a lack of faith.

This viral virus is a serious health concern for millions around the world. It is a virus which can easily spread. Because COVID-19 can be caught by tiny particles in the air, as well as by infected people and surfaces, many are starting to take heed to it.

I can recall months ago how some adolescent and young adults did not listen to the concerns of experts and local government officials. Some were holding various parties and gatherings though the pandemic is regarded as highly contagious. These young teenagers and adults have basically turned a blind eye to the warnings.

Now I do not condone the attitudes of young people who have basically thumbed their nose to the instructions of experts by carrying on as if a highly contagious infectious disease does not exist. What I do admire about some of the young men and women who have avoided the expert's warnings of not having large parties and gatherings is the fact that they are not obsessing over this pandemic. We all have an obligation to not allow the news of this viral outbreak to hinder our ability to enjoy life.

Although a carefree spirit is the mindset of many young people who choose to disregard the suggestions of experts and local officials, this mindset during this chaotic time can be both a blessing and a curse. One way that a carefree spirit can be viewed as a blessing is when an individual with that characteristic does not experience any worry or anxiety. Those who have that attitude are in the minority.

There are millions who are worried and filled with anxiety due to the amount of devastation that this virus has caused. So many people around the world cannot help but to become obsessed and have anxiety in regard to this epidemic, because they might not be able to pay their rent or mortgage as well as not having enough food to eat.

With the severity of this epidemic, it has literally become a matter of life or death.

In regard to the individual(s) with a carefree attitude, there is also a curse to having this particular mindset. The curse of those with a carefree spirit is that they are oblivious to the importance of taking an issue serious. If you have not heard the news by now, the COVID-19 virus must not be taken lightly.

One must strive to maintain a mental balance when it comes to this infectious disease. An individual should not become too carefree or too obsessed or worried. A healthy mental balance can be achieved when the individual does not allow this virus to constantly bombard one's mind.

Instead of worry and obsession over this pandemic, strive to fill your thoughts with love and healthiness. I believe that an individual who has these particular thoughts does not have any reason to obsess or worry. If one does not become obsessed over this viral trial, then one is victorious in this unprecedented challenge.

Everyone should know that the virus is serious, but it is unwise to obsess over it. Besides following all of the instructions of the experts, there is not anything else that one can do. Though it is beneficial to the individual, mentally, to not become overwhelmed and obsessed with the news and threat of this virus, it is also vital to do everything within one's power to also consider the outpouring of warnings.

In chapter one, I briefly discussed the law of attraction. I stated how thinking about something could come into full fruition when it is on your mind. For instance, an individual can speak something into existence, which commences in one's mind and thoughts.

Do not mistake me: I am not saying that an individual could ultimately become stricken with COVID-19 just by thinking about it. If that were the case, mostly every individual who is walking and breathing would become infected with it. The individual(s) with whom I am referring to is the man or woman who is fixated on becoming ill from this disease epidemic.

There are some individuals who falsely diagnose themselves with illnesses they are not suffering from. These particular individuals are commonly referred to as hypochondriacs. With the availability of the Internet, many are googling potential symptoms.

I believe that in some instances, looking up potential symptoms of an illness can make the individual worry even more. When COVID-19 commenced to be prevalent, I can recall how the virus was the most googled search on the Internet. There are some who have successfully diagnosed themselves online with the COVID-19 virus, while others were not so fortunate.

Contracting COVID-19 is a legitimate concern. What gets the majority of individuals in trouble in regard to becoming infected with the disease is the way in which the media is reporting on the continuous increase of individuals infected. The numbers are overwhelming, which could cause anyone to become filled with obsession and fear.

Though there is an alarming increase of this epidemic, an individual will do themselves a disservice by constantly allowing oneself to be fixated on this particular subject alone. Just because the pandemic is widespread and contagious does not mean that you will automatically fall ill to it. It is also wise to not let your guard down.

Thus far, I have been blessed and fortunate not to become affected by this perilous virus. One reason why I have been successful in not contracting the disease is because I pray each day on a continual basis. Secondly, I keep my mind on things that I deem enjoyable and positive.

When sports resumed, I can only imagine how it has helped youths, as well as men and women, clear their minds from the ongoing news coverage on COVID-19. Although the arenas and stadiums are not as filled to capacity as they once were before the spread of the virus, the resuming of these games can help an individual to not become obsessed over how dreadful the pandemic is. Sports have provided a way of escape from the troubles and issues in our new normal and everyday life.

Whether one is able to have an outlet through entertainment from the burdensome news of this pestilence or by becoming active in other activities, one must not become fixated or obsessed with this illness. Fixation about anything is never positive. If you do become fixated, hopefully it is on spiritual and mental wellness.

Before this pandemic became widespread, there were many who were not having a genuine and sincere relationship with the Creator. Some were only focusing on the material things in the world. Instead of setting their minds and hearts on the God of mercy and love, many chose to abandon Him.

When an individual has a relationship with the Father and the Son, there is not any need to become fearful and obsessive about what is occurring all around us. The Word of God is quite clear about the events that will happen in these last days. God's Word has accurately predicted that there will be pestilences (Matthew 24:7).

Those who do not read the Bible daily are the individuals who are likely to become worried and obsessed over this viral outbreak. Some who do not heed the warnings of God's Word have acted in shock and frustration over what was predicted to occur centuries ago. Now I am not saying that some followers of God do not also worry like other individuals who do not have a relationship with the Almighty, who is always correct in what He says.

This is the right time to turn to the heavenly Father. I am cognizant that thus far in this book, I have been primarily discussing how one should have a positive attitude and mindset in spite of the chaos and turmoil that this virus is causing. Sure, some have more optimism in life compared to others, but real joy and optimism that is long-standing and genuine only comes from referencing and acknowledging the Father.

It baffles me when some only turn to Him in a difficult crisis. Do not mistake me: God should be the One who we all depend upon in times of difficulty. Many use Him just to get by, then abandon Him when things return back to normal.

In regard to this perilous virus, I cannot confidently state that this nation, let alone the world, will ever return to the way it was. I believe that if we are blessed to find a reliable vaccine for this current virus, there might be another pestilence or situation which can also threaten the masses. No one can say with assurance that this country, as well as the world, will be able to escape other catastrophic and tragic events.

As humans, we tend to become focused on the wrong things. I understand that the COVID-19 virus has hurt and affected millions of lives. Instead of focusing and being obsessed with the potential of contracting this invisible disease, we all should aspire to focus on the Almighty.

There are a plethora of unnecessary cares in which many develop an unwanted obsession over. I am in no way saying that COVID-19 is something that should not be any cause for concern. Because there are so many lives affected in various ways, due to this epidemic, worry and obsession will become the eventual result.

Focusing on the Lord above will help to alleviate the obsession over this outbreak. It is always comforting when one has the confidence and faith that He is on your side. Is it difficult to trust that the Creator wants what is best for you? I hope that it is not difficult for you to realize that fact. The worst thing that one can do is turn this virus into an idol. When an individual obsesses over something, typically that issue or thing is basically a false god.

If an individual continues to live each day in the best way that one knows how, then that is all one could ask for. This particular virus does not care if you are a good person or a wicked individual; if it is meant for one to become infected with the pestilence, then it is out of one's control. Of course, I reiterate, everyone must continue to take precautions in regard to one's safety and also the safety of others.

Once you have carried out all the things that are required—for example, wearing masks in public and physical distancing—then you should not allow worry and obsession to have precedence in your life. There is always something that one could do to not allow this pandemic to dominate the mind. Though I am not a video-game fanatic, playing these games within reason could help an individual avoid obsession.

I am not suggesting that one replace one potential obsession with another. This is why I am saying that one play the games in a responsible fashion. Though many of us have a plethora of time to be indoors, it does not mean that one should play these video games twenty-four hours a day and seven days a week.

There are also an enormous amount of other activities which one can do in order to take one's mind off of the current state of our world and society. One activity that is always a good activity to do is solve puzzles. Puzzles are time-consuming. They require attention and focus of the mind.

Another activity, which is also an activity that is a necessity and is beneficial in the clearing of one's mind, is cleaning up the bedroom, bathroom, and living room. I know, for me, these activities alone require my undivided attention. Just because there is a pandemic does not mean that one should abandon regular house chores.

Also, another activity that is a classic activity, which you are doing now, is reading. There is nothing like reading a book, which can be beneficial in a couple of ways. One reason why reading a book is a great activity to help with the potential for obsession is it stimulates the mind and brain. Another benefit of reading is that it provides a positive way of escape.

I can recall how reading provided another outlet for me when I was a youth. If the book was interesting, I could not put it down. In these unprecedented times in which we live, reading could become the distraction that one needs to keep one's mind and thoughts off of obsession and worry.

The activities which I just discussed are some of the things that one could do to decrease one's obsession and fear. These activities will keep your mind busy without becoming worried. One can perform those activities without any pressure.

It is always soothing to listen to good music. Music that has a positive message can become motivating and reassuring. There is always a song which can help in these uncertain times.

Taking time away from the television is needed to become clear from obsession. Reading, cleaning, and playing on the computer does help provide a temporary relief. One should try to do these activities for sanity in the COVID-19 era.

Are you thankful to be alive? I hope that you are. This virus has claimed so many lives domestically and worldwide. It is definitely a situation that will strike fear in the most positive and optimistic individual.

Though it may be difficult to find the silver lining in regard to this pandemic, one must strive to approach each day with vigor and optimism. If one is not careful, the continuous coverage of this epidemic will consume one's mind. During this perilous and uncertain time, it is imperative that all who are living in the COVID-19 era take time to recognize how much of a blessing it is to face another day.

As long as you have your right mind, you are fortunate. In my opinion, it does not do the individual any good to complain and obsess over a virus we cannot physically control at this time. I am aware that this virus has caused a plethora of life-altering changes.

Because of this epidemic, one has to become cautious of positive greetings, such as hugs and handshakes. There are some families who can only see each other from a divided window. When it comes to visiting friends and loved ones, some complain and demonstrate disgust with lack of physical touch.

The positive way of looking at the scenario of lack of touching among stricken family members, who might be afflicted with the virus, is that physical separation and quarantining is for everyone's protection. Instead of understanding how physical distancing is beneficial in the long-term, many opt to obsessing over the fact that they cannot have face-to-face interaction with their loved ones and friends.

Recently I was asked about how I felt about the onset of this viral pandemic. The individual asked if I was fearful and worried about the threat of the pestilence. My response to the individual who posed the question was that it is an occurrence, although potentially deadly, in which we cannot live in the obsession and fear over it.

Obsessing and stressing over situations and circumstances which are beyond our control has no benefit. One must approach each day with thankfulness, not dread. I believe when an individual succumbs to dreading something, the situation will evolve into an unfortunate case of obsession and anxiety.

COVID-19 is an illness in which many are dreading will never affect them or those who hold a very special place in our lives. It seems as though the disease will destroy both the short-term and long-term health of any individual who happens to contract it. This is the very reason why many are obsessed and fearful of being stricken with the pestilence, even if they experience a mild form of the virus.

Now it is foolish for any individual living in the era of COVID-19 to not acknowledge the fact that it has negatively affected society. As a world and nation, we cannot continue to dread this unforeseen situation and circumstance. Dreading something in life could lead to more issues and problems that are unwanted. Living each day with thankfulness can influence one to curb their obsession.

I believe that when an individual becomes obsessed over something, that individual is at the mercy of it. One must not allow this virus to influence how one should live. What I mean is that one can still perform many of the activities they enjoyed pre-pandemic, but one must do those activities without recklessness.

My suggestion to everyone living in this era of unpredictability and uncertainty is to strive for peace and optimism. You cannot enjoy a life of calmness and hope when something is on your conscience. No one should ever allow this viral outbreak to stop one from living a life that is predicated on hope and joy.

When an individual obsesses over something, it is never good for the body. I am certain that there were plenty of individuals checking into various hospitals due to the frenzy over this epidemic. It could become detrimental to one's heart when worry and obsession is combined.

Unfortunately, obsession can very well manifest itself into reality. One has to be mindful of what they allow to have priority over one's heart and mind. This is why it is imperative to live each day without obsession and skepticism.

On one hand, I can understand how an individual's obsession with the COVID-19 virus could gradually enter into one's realm of thought. Our world and society has handled this epidemic from a worldly and earthly perspective. The world, in which we lived before this major outbreak, valued materialism over religion and spirituality.

In my opinion, God Almighty has allowed many to have obsessive thoughts over the potential threat of becoming infected with this uncontrollable viral foe. Instead of trusting the fact that He can and will protect individuals by not allowing the disease to wreak havoc on the mind, some chose to surrender to fear and negative thoughts. This virus has really revealed where one's true heart lies.

Prioritizing the threat of this virus over a deep and meaningful prayer life is not a wise way to alleviate falling victim to obsessive thoughts about becoming afflicted with the infectious disease. Now is the time to call upon the Creator. I do not profess to know how He will answer you when you come to Him, but I do know that He can give you the peace of mind to carry on in life despite what is going on in the world and society due to this pandemic.

There are many who fear the unknown. Because we as humans have a natural tendency to want to know every aspect of our lives, the majority of us cannot handle unpredictability and uncertainty. Sometimes an individual might fear the unknown situations that will ultimately come into fruition.

The COVID-19 virus has inadvertently caused our world and nation to become fully invested in obsession. Hopefully, in the near future, the world's obsession will become obsolete. Only a reliable vaccine and a decrease in the number of fatalities stemming from the virus can cure the COVID-19 obsession. When the masses are living in a state of obsession, there is always a cause for concern.

Joy and happiness cannot blossom in an individual's life when one is fixated and obsessed over a particular situation or circumstance. COVID-19 has turned many individuals' smiles into frowns. It is as though this virus became a cloud of darkness over the world.

Our nation has endured great chaos and turmoil due to this outbreak. When you go out in public, you can tell how everyone is on edge. One can come to the conclusion that the reason why some are psychologically affected by this horrendous pandemic is because of the panic that this disease has caused.

As a result of the obsession of the masses, many are acting in frantic ways. There are some who are so infatuated with the threat of this virus that their actions and behaviors are suspect. For example, there is not any need to buy out all the essential products in which everyone needs.

Due to the obsessive nature of many, shelves at local grocers and supermarkets are bare. Some are so filled with worry and anxiety that as a result, these individuals are stockpiling on numerous amounts of items. I can recall how at the genesis of this pandemic, many were buying water and toilet paper as if there would not be any tomorrow.

In my opinion, this pestilence has turned into mass hysteria. This is why the majority of people are behaving out of their minds. Many are so fearful and worried about today that they are oblivious of what could happen the next day. When obsession gives way to fear, then erratic behavior has the potential of occurring.

We all must strive to minimize fear and obsession in our lives. The best thing that one can do is, do those things which makes you feel happy and comfortable. There is nothing more than an individual living in the COVID-19 era should do in order to maintain and sustain one's happiness and sanity.

An individual who allows their joy to become taken away really does not have consistency in one's outlook. Sadly, many are yielding to fear and obsession because they do not know how to respond and react to this epidemic. Personally, I have learned that an individual is a catastrophic event away from losing one's mind.

With the obsessive and hysterical behavior of many in our world and society, it remains to be seen if some will ultimately remain stagnate in the current state they are presently in. At this present moment, I am unsure how an individual's obsession could eventually turn into peace and joy. Although hysteria and obsession over this pandemic has not currently lost its momentum, as an individual living in the midst of this viral outbreak, I still personally have hope that, one day, all diseases and pestilences in our world will no longer become a threat physically or mentally.

The COVID-19 virus is more than an obsession. It has manifested itself into our everyday way of living. We all must accept the fact that this virus could perhaps become a constant issue in the world we live.

Those suffering with mental health issues are in a precarious position. They have to try to maintain a positive mental mindset in the midst of a devastating infectious disease. Also, some who are faced with psychological conditions might not be able to have face-to-face interaction with their psychiatrist or therapist.

I believe that mental health cases have increased due to the obsession over this viral threat. One's mind can take a beating when all an individual hears about daily is how many are perishing from an uncontrollable infectious disease. Hearing negativity on a continuous basis can weigh heavily on an individual's mind, especially when one is affected by a psychological illness.

When an individual who is suffering from a psychological disorder becomes obsessed with an issue, such as the COVID-19 pandemic, it is definitely a cause for concern. An individual who is bearing a mental disorder does not need to experience any added-on stress. Unfortunately, some who are mentally ill will not become able to thrive mentally because of this worldwide obsession.

Many of the psychiatrists and therapists are only seeing established patients. Furthermore, some of these mental health professionals are doing virtual appointments only. One who is affected by a psychological disorder are at a disadvantage due to the closing of the offices of doctors and therapists who would normally help individuals who are in dire need.

I am saddened by the lack of available help for the mentally ill. This does not mean that there is not any help or support for individuals struggling mentally at all, but before the pandemic, there was more availability of doctors and therapists to those coping with a mental illness. It is one thing for an individual who is not affected with a mental disorder to experience fear and obsession from the spread of the virus, but fear and obsession for the bearer of a psychological condition is even more damaging and severe.

In regard to every individual's mental health, it is imperative that the individual do everything that one can to maintain it. Though it can become difficult to have a clear mind in this era of COVID-19, I believe that it is possible to develop and have a calm countenance.

If one's mental state is positive, then there will not be any semblance of mental agony.

Focusing on one's mental health can prove beneficial in these uncertain times. When your mind is calm, obsessive thoughts will not have any effect. Right now, it might seem that one does not have any choice in allowing the news of this pandemic to saturate one's mind and thoughts.

Living one's life in constant obsession is never a life that is fulfilled. If you can, aspire to remain calm and positive in spite of the continuous obsession with the COVID-19 viral pandemic. In order to sustain overall wellness, do not surrender to obsession.

CHAPTER 4

Anticipate Good Health

Death is something that many would rather avoid. COVID-19 has the majority of individuals questioning their own mortality. Because of the damage that this virus has caused in the healthiest of people, many are concerned about their overall physical health and wellness.

The experts on the COVID-19 virus determined that there are factors in an individual's health which could contribute to one perishing from the virus. One factor that experts initially stated would be cause for concern if one happens to become infected with the virus is obesity. A second factor that the experts deemed another important physical health contributor to succumbing to this viral pestilence is diabetes.

Although there are some individuals who have perished from this deadly virus with no known underlying health issues, the overwhelming majority of victims of this deadly epidemic suffered from health conditions, such as heart disease and obesity. Individuals who are bearers of these health illnesses which I have just mentioned are most likely to perish from COVID-19. This is definitely a cause for concern for many individuals, particularly in the United States.

For decades, this country has enjoyed having an abundance of food. Compared to other nations, America has not had any lack in regard to food insecurity. As a result of this country's fascination and obsession with fast food, many of its citizens have developed numerous health conditions.

Before the onset of the COVID-19 virus, America as a whole needed to become healthy physically. Obesity and a lack of a reasonable exercise regimen has resulted in illnesses which have the potential to shorten one's life. COVID-19 is another health concern that many with physical illnesses as a result of poor eating and exercise habits must also consider.

Now I am not stating that individuals who happen to have physical health issues and conditions cannot survive becoming afflicted with this invisible illness. There have been instances in which individuals with underlying health issues have combated and beaten the virus. Most experts would agree that the more physically fit that an individual is, the greater of a chance that individual's body can fight off the viral disease.

If one happens to contract the virus, anticipate health and strength instead of perishing from it. Though this viral outbreak has resulted in sorrow in the lives of many, there are also some success stories. When any individual hears of someone who has overcome any type of illness or sickness, it is always a reason for hope.

Good physical health should become the goal for all living in the COVID-19 era. Individuals who are well physically can also enjoy overall wellness of health. One must do everything in one's power to maintain good overall health despite the continuous increase in the COVID-19 virus.

Becoming physically healthy during this chaotic time can become difficult for some. The pressure of maintaining a household and sustaining one's overall health is not easy. Some would have a routine of exercising in the gym before this pandemic hit.

There are some exercise establishments which are open for business, but I am unsure if these gyms are completely safe from the spread of the virus. I understand how some of the members of the staff of these gyms wipe down the exercise equipment as well as taking the temperature of its gym members. Personally, I believe that it is a potential risk for the staff of these exercise establishments, and also the patrons, to continue to have the establishment open for business.

Presently, due to the concern of contracting the COVID-19 virus, many are opting out of gym memberships. Of course, I do not blame them. This viral disease can live on surfaces for a substantial period of time.

Although it is not feasible to exercise in a gym due to the virus, one must discover other creative ways to maintain a healthy weight. I believe that it is more beneficial to work out indoors, in the comfort of one's home, as opposed to exercising at an exercise establishment where the virus might lurk. Psychologically, working out at home is not as mentally challenging as exercising elsewhere.

Your health is extremely vital in life. Without good and adequate health, an individual will not have an enjoyable life of quality. It is unfortunate that some with challenging health issues have lives which consist of doctors and hospital visits.

The pandemic has forced many to spend a plethora of time in area hospitals. It goes beyond whether or not an individual exercises in a home gym or an established one. If an individual is unfortunately infected with the viral disease, it is imperative that the individual focuses on becoming mentally and physically whole.

COVID-19 is a disease which has the potential to be overcome. Sure, one's chance of recovery is greater when the individual is already physically fit. Realistically, it should not take a viral outbreak in order for one to take one's physical health seriously.

A lesson for many living in this era of COVID-19 is to never put your health on the backburner. Physical and mental health is more valuable now because of the onset of this viral infectious disease. An individual who contracts the virus will typically have a greater advantage in combating the virus if one's health is up to par.

I am cognizant of the fact that this disease affects both the health-conscious individual as well as the less physically active one. It is imperative that each individual living during this pandemic aspires to have a health routine despite this outbreak. Though physical fitness does not automatically stop someone from contracting the virus, in many cases, I believe that it ultimately helps.

As time progresses, hopefully there will be answers in the solving of this mysterious pestilence. In the meantime, it is vital that each man, woman, and child does what is necessary to develop good health. Practicing good eating habits and having a healthy diet plan are just a few of the things that one can do to increase one's chances of fighting and defeating this invisible foe if one happens to become a victim of it.

This virus attacks an individual physically, but it all commences in one's mind. The physical effects of the COVID-19 virus can weigh heavily on an individual's mental health and stability. If one is not mentally strong and fit, this virus could negatively affect one's mind.

The symptoms of COVID-19 can become extremely unbearable. Excruciating headaches, uncontrollable shaking, and vomiting might have the most mentally stable individual break down mentally. Also, hearing about all the deaths which have resulted from this viral outbreak could cause an individual who is infected with the pestilence to become overwhelmed with anxiety and fear.

I believe that an individual's overall health is sustained when one's body is whole from head to toe. COVID-19 threatens an individual's ability to cognitively process what is happening to them physically. While in the midst of the burdensome pain of this disease, the infected individual becomes occupied with trying to find relief from the illness.

When this worldwide epidemic initially became widespread, I could not have imagined how the importance of an individual's mental outlook would come at the forefront. It requires an enormous amount of strength, physically and mentally, in order to defeat this invisible invader of health. As the rise in fatalities from the COVID-19 virus increases, some might suggest that there is currently little hope for the individual who becomes stricken.

It must be intimidating to an individual's overall psyche after learning how this illness could potentially end one's life. This is why I wholeheartedly believe that the mind definitely factors into one's chances of survival. If one thinks, within his or her mind, that the virus will end their time on earth, then sadly, there is potential that this could come into reality.

Individuals who have survived being infected with the COVID-19 virus are brave and courageous. I cannot fathom why the stricken individual would not be. Overcoming a major viral disease with limited remedies and vaccines to presently cure it is definitely amazing.

In this life, we cannot all experience material wealth. Sometimes the riches in this life cannot buy someone good health. No one can enjoy one's wealth without some semblance of wellness.

The COVID-19 viral pandemic has destroyed the lives of both the fortunate and less fortunate alike. This virus is not concerned about economic and financial stability. A sound mind is more important to an individual's health than the accumulation of possessions and riches.

One cannot have good overall health without having a sound mind. The mind can influence the rest of the body to shut down. Therefore, it is extremely important how an individual's overall mindset is when one does unfortunately contract COVID-19.

Hopefully you will not become stricken with the illness, but if you do contract it, strive to tell yourself positive things. For example, while battling it, you could envision surviving it. Your mind could become the gateway for improved health over this viral epidemic.

Battling the COVID-19 virus could become an uphill battle for some. Not only does the individual infected have to endure all the side effects as a result of this potentially debilitating illness, but chances are that the individual who suffered from the disease may never return back to the individual they were before becoming infected.

Some cannot deal with the decline of their physical health. It has been discovered that some individuals who have been stricken with COVID-19 are still feeling the same symptoms from the disease after several months. I can imagine the stricken individual, who is still experiencing lingering and painful effects of the virus, asking themselves, "When will this ever end?" As of now, experts are uncertain about how long an individual who is infected long-term with COVID-19 will have to continue in suffering.

What this epidemic ultimately boils down to is patience, both mentally and physically. One cannot disregard how patience is needed when trying to recover from any type of traumatic experience. This pestilence, though quite concerning, is still a relatively new infectious disease.

Though there are currently new vaccines available for some in regard to this viral threat, only front line health workers and those who live in nursing homes—like the elderly—are given the green light to take the now-available vaccine. As I am writing this book, there is still a great amount of people perishing from COVID-19, but because of the development of these new vaccines, some are remaining hopeful that the number of individuals perishing from the virus will be on the decline. The vaccines for COVID-19 could not have come at a better time.

My hope for the world and this nation is that many return to a healthy state, both mentally and physically. In the coming months, there is a chance that the health of many could be restored. Time and patience are essential to learning what these new vaccines can do in the prevention and treatment of the COVID-19 virus.

For many people, especially when it comes to the new vaccines, it's basically a wait-and-see approach to the potency and efficacy of these treatments. In communities of color, there is already a built-in mistrust of experimental treatments and vaccines, dating back to previous decades. If these vaccines can be relied upon in the near future, then there will be many who will become fortunate enough to experience health, which is more valuable than gold or precious pearls.

Mental mindsets are important, especially in the era of COVID-19. Although, it is difficult to fully prepare for becoming ill with the virus, one can learn how to adjust mentally to it. How does one adjust to a life-threatening illness? Honestly, the only way in which one can adjust one's mental mindset in becoming afflicted with the viral disease is by gradually chipping away at the disease.

Every day is not the same. There are good days and bad days. One's ultimate goal and mindset should be the defeat of the virus and the individual's overall wellness.

Becoming physically well from this virus typically does not occur for some. Some individuals who are infected with this pestilence are asymptomatic. This means that the individual who tests positive for the virus are not experiencing any symptoms.

In other words, these particular individuals may have the virus, but they are not physically affected by it. Asymptomatic individuals could become harmful to others. Usually, those who are asymptomatic are unaware that they are carriers of the COVID-19 illness.

For the individual who experiences the disease with little to no symptoms, there is not any need to adjust one's mental mindset. In most cases, the asymptomatic individual can usually resume regular activities. It is the individual who is severely stricken that must somehow develop a positive and patient mindset.

When a severely stricken individual with the COVID-19 virus views it as a long-term battle, he or she can strive for getting better one day at a time. The mindset of "chipping away" at the virus demonstrates that type of mentality. Sometimes an individual who prepares to have a lengthy battle with a particular illness could surprise themselves, as well as the doctors, by having a speedy recovery.

A positive mindset is just as important as physical health. Without commencing mentally with a vision of physical wholeness, the mind cannot instruct the other parts of the body to perform. Many take the mind as an illegitimate nonfactor in overcoming illnesses, which are damaging to one's physical capabilities.

I cannot reiterate and stress enough how one's mental and internal makeup can become a lifeline to capabilities that one thought they could not have achieved. This reminds me of athletes who physically push themselves to the limit. Many successful ones might not possess the physical attributes of other athletes in their same and respective sport, but the athlete with mental grit and toughness will gradually chip away at becoming an outstanding performer in spite of having lesser physical gifts.

In regard to winning the battle over the COVID-19 virus, an individual who is supposedly physically healthy pre-positive COVID-19 test for the virus could fare poorly over an individual with underlying health issues who has the right mentality to overcome the condition. The individual with patience and determination can successfully recover from a potentially life-threatening virus.

Self-pity will destroy an individual's recovery to health. Feeling sympathy toward oneself impedes the process of acquiring good health because the individual with that mindset will usually remain stagnate. Those who demonstrate self-pity are essentially conceding to something.

In regard to the COVID-19 virus, many are wallowing in pity. Some of these individuals have yielded to the virus, thus throwing in the towel. Presently, it is a mystery how some can be afflicted with the disease and feeling well, while others who are also afflicted are struggling to live.

Now I do not condone an individual who is suffering from a life-threatening virus to try to take on the persona that they are strong and not any need of consoling. It is unrealistic to think that an individual who is stricken with COVID-19 will not struggle with testing positive for the virus. What I am saying is that once someone learns of one's diagnosis, it should not automatically cause that individual to lay down and die, or in other words, give up.

The mindset of an individual battling COVID-19 must be optimistic. At least an optimistic attitude can give the individual infected with the illness a greater chance of recovery. I believe that some individuals with an attitude of self-pity do not ever anticipate becoming healthy again.

Yes, I am aware that the increase in COVID-19 has taken the lives of many unsuspecting individuals. No one in one's right mind sets out to become ill from this pestilence. If you or someone you love becomes stricken with the COVID-19 virus, encouragement instead of self-pity is needed.

Please do not fall into the mindset of self-pity, which could basically have a domino effect on one's overall health. When an individual chooses to have a self-pity mindset, that person is acknowledging defeat. Subconsciously, an individual affected by any illness who chooses to have a mindset of self-pity is essentially telling the sickness before the battle begins, "You win!"

Every individual in the world is battling the COVID-19 virus in some way. One way in which we are all battling the virus is by taking all the necessary precautions to ward against it. Of course, we are also fighting the virus battle internally and mentally.

Battling this perilous virus mentally can become mentally exhausting. When one is exhausted mentally, there is a tendency for that individual to resort to self-pity. This mindset is detrimental to someone's physical recovery and mental growth.

This invisible threat has forced everyone living in this present time to remain vigilant. There is not any way that one can remain alert in this physical and mental battle with COVID-19 by having a self-pity and defeatist mindset and attitude. Our overall physical and mental health is at stake, and self-pity will always threaten it.

Maintaining and sustaining good health is extremely vital in an individual's life. Without consistency in health, that individual has a greater chance of perishing. Now is the time to consider one's options in regard to health.

I believe the worst thing that an individual can do in these stressful and uncertain times is binge and stress eat. It is very unhealthy to eat while we are stressed because it leads to obesity and weight gain. When it comes to the threat of the COVID-19 virus, it is better to not become concerned with additional health conditions.

Eating healthy is increasingly becoming difficult. We all must become creative in our food choices because with the shelves in most local grocery markets being emptied each day, some do not have the luxury of food options. Sadly, many of us must make do with what we can get.

If one is lucky enough to get a product in the grocery store, that item might be more expensive due to the demand of the product. Water is an essential product in which we all cannot live without. It is a requirement to our overall health that one consumes and enjoys this particular beverage.

Although I am no health expert, I have seen many individuals in local markets stock up on sodas and cold drinks rather than water. Too much soda could have a negative effect on one's body and health. As an individual's health is compromised, the less likely the individual could potentially combat the virus.

With the threat of COVID-19, one must strive to be at one's optimum health. Acquiring good eating habits may not stop an individual from coming down with any type of illness, but it gives that person a fighting chance if an illness ever occurs. One has to have a certain mindset when it comes to health and food.

COVID-19 has been the antithesis in regard to good health. It seems as though this virus will destroy an individual's overall health if it is not combated with a competent medical staff. This is why it is imperative that the individual do all that is within one's realm of power to practice all the health precautions.

I understand how an individual might become frustrated with having to be cognizant continuously with one's overall health. If becoming aware of your health helps you with not perishing from this infectious disease, then embrace the concern. It is better to have concern for one's overall health rather than disregard the concern, which could result in deterioration.

Though the COVID-19 virus is potentially deadly, there is hope that one could still enjoy good health after contracting it. In the era of COVID-19, health and wellness is not at all assured. It does not require an individual with a great amount of understanding to realize that fact. One must never disregard how vital health can become to every member of the community.

Diseases and pestilences have threatened the health of many members of society for centuries. Each time that an epidemic has plagued a society, precious lives were lost, thus threatening the morale and overall health of many. The COVID-19 pandemic threat will hopefully become solved in due time.

What can we do as a nation and society to have those living in it experience overall wellness? One thing we can do is continue to follow what the experts on infectious diseases suggest what we must do. I believe the best way that one is guaranteed good health in this pandemic era is by wearing masks each time that one has to go out in public, physical distancing, and eliminating any significant type of social gatherings. There are millions of Americans who are putting their health, as well as the overall health of others, in jeopardy because they long for social interaction.

I believe that sacrificing interaction with others for the sake of one's health is definitely vital and beneficial long-term. As a culture, many of us desire immediate results. Patience is viewed as the enemy, particularly in regard to limiting the spread of COVID-19.

As I am writing this book, I could not have helped but to notice how so many people are not viewing the wearing of the masks and physical distancing as a necessity for health. When an individual is consistent in following all the protocols and precautions, then one can feel more secure mentally. Currently, as a nation, there is a spike in the number of COVID-19 cases and deaths because many have become lax and complacent.

In order for the United States to experience a decline in deaths and an increase in overall health, we all must learn how to have discipline. There are few who are holding individuals accountable who do not want to comply with the suggested precautions given by experts and government officials. As a result, the whole community and nation suffers.

The goal for this country should be for all of its citizens to not have to become worried or concerned about the potential of perishing from the virus. There is a lesser chance of that happening when the country as a whole commits to making health and wellness a top priority. We live in a democracy in America, which can also influence some to make the decision not to prioritize physical and mental health and wellness.

Good health and overall wellness should not become political. In this era of the COVID-19 pandemic, premium health is desired by all regardless of one's political party affiliation. When the issue of health in regard to COVID-19 is universally viewed as important, then progress can be made and accomplished.

It is foolish to not desire to have good health. When the masses are putting themselves and others in potential danger by minimizing the importance of the safety precautions in place, then essentially they are acting in apathy. In regard to one's health, there is not any middle ground.

A healthy mind and body is needed in this invisible fight. There are many who desire to become healthy, but for some reason, these individuals are allowing this virus to dictate their level of fitness. For instance, young and mature people alike are packing on what is called "the quarantine 15."

What the "quarantine 15" means is the individual has gained at least fifteen pounds due to inactivity from not exercising during quarantine, and it can also be attributed to stress eating. If one is fortunate enough to still live in the home in which one resided in before the outbreak of this pandemic, then that individual can still remain physically active. Previously, I discussed how one could get creative in regard to exercising.

Some do not have exercise equipment at home because they relied on an exercise gym for physical fitness. I do know of some people who have resumed their workouts in the exercise establishment, but in the era of COVID-19, exercising in public could pose a greater risk of contracting COVID-19 as opposed to exercising in the friendly confines of home. Remaining active while being at home should not become difficult to do.

I have seen exercise gurus demonstrate how an individual can still remain active at home. There are items in which one can use to substitute for weights. Lifting big jugs of water can be just as effective as lifting weights in a random exercise gym.

I believe that if you have walking steps where you reside or a backyard, then you can still get a feasible workout. The COVID-19 virus is not an excuse to become lazy or lethargic. In fact, this is the right time to become healthy, while prioritizing one's physical and mental health.

If you do not become physically active and fit now, then I do not foresee any other opportunity to become fit. Because one is in control of what one would prefer to do while at home, it is not a far stretch to incorporate exercise into one's daily routine. Exercising is good for the mind and brain.

A healthy mind is both crucial and beneficial to one's overall mood. When an individual chooses to have a daily exercise regimen while indoors due to this virus, typically one will be in such a positive and optimistic mood that the continuous coverage on this pandemic will not have any long-term effect, both mentally and physically. One advantage of exercising while at home is the easy access to Vitamin D. The only thing that an individual living at home can do to receive their dose of this vitamin is walk outdoors in one's backyard or patio.

In order to continue to maintain a positive mood in the era of COVID-19, spending brief periods outdoors in the sunlight can significantly affect your overall mood and outlook. COVID-19 has caused many to evaluate how healthy they are. My suggestion is to continue to remain active the best way that you know how. No one can afford to become irresponsible in regard to one's overall wellness and health.

Developing a healthy lifestyle in this era of COVID-19 can be acquired. It will require commitment and patience. If you need to regain control over your health, do not hesitate to do it.

At the rate in which this epidemic is progressing, the chances of someone becoming infected with the virus might seem inevitable. Thus far, I have discussed how vital precautions are in the prevention of the spread of COVID-19. In my opinion, the wearing of masks, as well as regularly washing one's hands, is promoting good hygiene.

Hygiene and health are definitely intertwined. When an individual does not practice sound hygiene, usually sickness is the result. Think about this virus: it typically spreads when someone touches another individual or a surface which is infected then, shortly thereafter, touches one's face, nose, or mouth.

The COVID-19 virus can become neutralized with good hygiene habits. Due to the fear of contracting the disease, products that are used for cleaning is flying off the shelves. This reveals the importance of cleanliness in our lives.

My mother has been a woman of cleanliness from as early as I can remember. Before the outbreak of this worldwide pandemic, she always suggested to myself, as well as to close friends and family members, that we should wash our hands. Though the COVID-19 virus is not a laughing matter, I was personally amused when the experts revealed the importance of washing one's hands in the initial requirements and guidelines in combating the viral epidemic.

The reason why I was so amused by the initial instructions of the experts suggesting that we wash our hands is because my late grandfather would poke fun at my mother for stressing to him how hygienic it is to handwash. He would yell out to my mother in sarcasm, "Wash your hands!" Years later, I never knew that a harmless joke would one day become one of the vital factors in preventing the spread of a highly contagious viral pestilence.

Unfortunately, there are a plethora of individuals who do not give credence to being clean and hygienic. Some still cough and sneeze without covering their mouth and nose. This is why face coverings and masks must be worn indefinitely at this present time.

It is more than just a rude gesture to cough and sneeze without covering one's mouth, but it is also the health and livelihood of an individual that is at stake. We all know by now that the COVID-19 virus can be spread by tiny particles in the air from a potential individual who is infected with the disease. Talking, coughing, sneezing, and yelling are normal things in which any individual does during a course of a day, but these normal things which are performed by just about everyone could become a contributing factor in spreading and contracting COVID-19. The wearing of a mask, generally, protects everyone's health and well-being, although it can become highly uncomfortable to wear at times.

When an individual exercises, washes one's hands, wears the face coverings, and physically distances oneself, that individual has essentially participated, health-wise, in the prevention of this deadly disease. Following those guidelines could result in continual health. After one follows the guidelines and protocols for good health in the COVID-19 era, one must think healthy, not sickly.

CHAPTER 5

Take Life as It Comes

One thing that I have learned to appreciate is life. This viral pandemic has influenced me personally to not sweat the small stuff. With the uncontrollable spread of the COVID-19 virus, each day that you are alive must become savored.

There is a great amount of serious issues besides the pandemic that is wreaking havoc in our country. It is difficult to experience optimism and joy when the next day is not promised. In regard to the uncertainty of life, it is imperative that each living and breathing human being takes the time to cherish each day in which one does have here on earth.

We all can find optimism and some semblance of joy in the midst of these turbulent and chaotic times. Due to the onset of COVID-19, many are not motivated to identify the joy in their lives. Many are experiencing life but not living it.

Every individual has life experiences. Some experiences in life are either positive or negative. Mentally and internally, we tend to define our lives by our own experiences in life.

In this era of COVID-19, some are allowing this disease to determine their amount of happiness and joy. Depression and anxiety is prevalent among the majority of individuals living in these unprecedented times. The COVID-19 pandemic has essentially held many captive in their negative thoughts and feelings.

Is life today like it was at this present time two to five years ago? I can confidently say, "Of course not!" No one can decide which situations and circumstances one will encounter. That is up to the Creator above.

Life must be received, whether the times are filled with the abundance of joy or the pain, agony, and disappointment which every one of us will ultimately experience at some point. The COVID-19 virus pandemic is a situation and circumstance that has resulted in pain and sorrow. An optimistic individual does not disregard how hard a trial is in one's life; that person will continue to live through that painful ordeal while hoping for a better tomorrow.

Individuals living in the COVID-19 era should strive to live each day with joy. Happiness comes and goes, but joy is always long-standing. Things might go awry in life, but the individual with joy can withstand unfavorable situations and occurrences.

What kind of individual do you consider yourself to be? Is your joy at a standstill because there is so much devastation in our world and nation due to the COVID-19 viral pandemic? If the joy of living turns into deep anxiety and depression, then your joy is not solid. Joy is demonstrated when the individual can view each day with the same anticipation and enthusiasm as the previous one. I understand how this virus could affect the ability of an individual to have sustainable joy because the COVID-19 pandemic has put a damper on the livelihoods of millions of individuals worldwide.

Can you honestly say that you are happy to be alive? With the COVID-19 virus, there are some who would prefer not to live another day. These individuals only enjoy life when there are no trials to encounter. Individuals who do not yield to ending one's life because life might become unbearable must be commended.

Due to the enormous amount of people perishing from this epidemic, some might question their life's purpose. It is not easy to live when those closest to you are severely and, perhaps, permanently affected by this viral threat. In the lifetimes of the majority of individuals, we have never experienced a viral pandemic of this magnitude.

One might ask oneself, "When will this nightmare end?" No one can confidently predict when the world, collectively will be able to gain control over the spread of this virus. While the nation and the world are aspiring to decrease the astronomical numbers of victims of this epidemic, the world is still in motion. As a valued member of society, your life should not be viewed as unimportant.

To all the individuals who have perished or have been physically affected by COVID-19, life matters. Every individual, regardless of how long one lives numerically, must be happy and thankful for another precious day. This is the reason why we must appreciate all seasons in the spectrums of life.

In this life, no one can boast about a problem-free life. The COVID-19 virus has brought the various issues of life right into the forefront. For example, the issue of death has become the leading topic of discussion in many households worldwide.

When we take life as it comes, we become fully aware that death is a natural part of life's cycle. Now I am not trying to minimize death, but although it is inevitable for most, it is more imperative that one enjoys life until one's number is called. This does not mean that one should actively seek death.

Instead of pursuing death because of lack of hope in life, one must be courageous enough to accept all of the highs and lows in which life entails. Sure, the COVID-19 virus has emerged as a physical and psychological issue in our world and society, but it should not give anyone living in this present time a reason not to face this epidemic in the way in which other health conditions of concern were ultimately dealt with in the past. Health issues which were plaguing our world and society in past decades have been able to become resolved through tireless research and trials.

Every so often in life, there has been, throughout the decades, a pestilence or health condition that has threatened the very fabric of society. These medical plagues, which now includes COVID-19, have always had the potential of affecting the quality of life of many. One must become mindful that these diseases and pestilences will always occur in our world and society, but there is always hope that when these pestilences do occur, there can be some type of relief. While we anticipate relief from this pandemic, do not forget to live in the meanwhile.

Accepting the fact that the COVID-19 virus might be here to stay in our world and society could become difficult for some to accept. This virus, whether one is accepting of it or not, is playing a significant role in the lives of every individual. Illnesses and diseases are an unfortunate reality of life.

Though pestilences are never easy to endure, because we live in a fallen world, they will occur. As a member of society, it is imperative that one accepts all the problems and issues, which is a part of it. COVID-19 is an illness in our world that requires both a proactive and patient approach.

This approach is a microcosm of what life entails. There are times in life in which one must aggressively pursue a goal or an opportunity. As the goal is pursued, patience of the goal coming into fruition is the final step.

In regard to the COVID-19 virus, we must accept the fact that it will not subside unless every individual in our society, proactively and aggressively, does what is required of them. What I mean by proactively carrying out the requirements of this life-altering disease is what all the experts are saying. One must continue to wear the face coverings, physical distance, and of course, wash one's hands thoroughly.

After these requirements are proactively practiced, the result of one's effort should yield to a positive result. Just like most things in life, the fruit of one's effort requires time and patience. I cannot speak about other cultures and societies, but in the United States, many of its citizens are not as patient as one would prefer them to be.

Many in this society would like to reap the benefits of the desired results, but do not want to do what is required to achieve them. When members of society cannot follow instructions, then society as a whole will not benefit. Also, the quality of life in that society will also suffer and become greatly affected.

As I previously stated, life must be lived, not just experienced. This virus has been just that, a negative experience. Some feel that they cannot comfortably live their lives due to this viral catastrophe.

Sadly, some individuals in our society will never take heed to what is required by wise experts in regard to this viral pandemic. I have learned from this viral outbreak that there are two types of individuals in life. One type of individual is receptive to life's challenges, while the other type of individual complains and acts defiantly.

What about you? Do you fall into the category of the individuals who I just discussed? In my opinion, complaining and noncompliance is not an ideal way to deal with this infectious disease epidemic. Individuals who consciously decide to become difficult and defiant in regard to all the guidelines and protocols concerning the COVID-19 pandemic are not only hurting others, but they are also inadvertently doing harm to themselves as well.

The individual who is receptive to life's challenges and difficulties accepts whatever comes one's way. I am aware of how difficult it can become to welcome change. This virus has left many without a choice but to embrace the new normal in our world. Life will continue whether one is on board with the process or not.

Resilience from this tragic pestilence must be the direction of our world and nation. In previous years, America has bounced back from numerous catastrophic events. This country has proven in the past that it can recover from whatever negative situation or circumstance that is thrown its way.

This nation and other countries in the world have encountered and endured events, which will have one questioning if it is realistic that recovery is in the near future. In the United States alone, there has been tragedy after tragedy, which has brought this nation to the brink of constant sorrow. Life has dealt this once great nation a significant blow when the virus initially swept throughout all fifty states.

As a nation, we cannot wallow in defeat and self-pity. These attitudes and mindsets threaten the core and the fabric of what America stood for in previous years. I have seen this nation take a significant hit while pressing on.

The United States has taken a tragic hit in every aspect of life. The COVID-19 virus has unveiled how this nation is on the brink of utter destruction domestically. This country is reeling from the economic and financial burden that has resulted from the uncontrollable spread of this invisible foe.

Life for many in this country has gotten difficult to navigate through. Instead of resiliency, I have seen pain and defeat in the faces of many. Some are not confident that America can recover from this negative occurrence this time.

Now I cannot predict if the country can universally recover, but I believe that it is up to each individual to have an optimistic perspective on life. Because many cannot rely upon wealth and riches, there are other things in life that should be of more significance. So many people are affected financially from the closing of businesses that they now are struggling with understanding the meaning of why they must endure these trials which have come upon them.

We must all decide in our minds and hearts that giving up on life is never an option. One must come to the realization that life is more than just finances. In the ever-changing process of life, riches and financial stability are not always constant.

Ultimately, we all must choose what is important in our lives. COVID-19 has forced many to prioritize life rather than trivial issues. Today many are trying to remain healthy and survive this current pestilence.

Each day, in which we are fortunate enough to become a part of, is a chance for an individual to become better as a person. With the uncertainty of life, as well as this unprecedented virus, it is wise to aspire to become as positive in regard to life as possible. We must leave yesterday behind and strive to improve upon the next day. Doctors and experts striving to come up with a remedy for the COVID-19 virus are also looking to improve the lives of millions.

No one could have predicted that millions would become affected by this global pandemic. After the chaos and turmoil of this mysterious virus ensued, life has drastically changed. We do not have the freedom to currently do some of the activities in which we previously enjoyed.

Due to the spread of the COVID-19 virus, activities such as going to the cinema and shopping at the local shopping center has somewhat been essentially phased out. Instead of interacting with others, computers and phones have replaced interpersonal face time.

Schools and universities have gone to virtual learning as an option to in-person classes.

These are just a few changes which are now a huge part of our everyday lives. In some instances, some have not been able to have an option to change. It is as though these changes have been thrust upon some individuals.

Unfortunately, many of us do not have any choice but to accept the changes in one's life due to the spread of COVID-19. Complaining and holding a grudge does not do anyone living in these times any good. Life is still in progress, so one would want to also adapt to whatever comes one's way.

Some individuals do themselves a disservice by avoiding change in one's life. The COVID-19 virus has forced many in the masses to become adaptable. Though adapting to change might initially become a problem for some, it is basically something that life encompasses.

Eventually we all will get used to the ongoing process of change as a result of this pandemic. There are always pros and cons in regard to change. One must not focus on the challenges.

The only thing that an individual can do when facing challenges such as this is face them head on. It serves no purpose to avoid and run from them. When it comes to the COVID-19 virus, we as a society must not sweep this health issue under the rug. Issues that are not tackled full steam ahead will still remain and, in most cases, eventually worsen.

If you are an old soul or a seasoned adult, then you are aware of how there are various life cycles in life. Sometimes one will experience a negative or tough cycle, and then in other times in life, that cycle is easy and smooth. When it comes to the COVID-19 virus, we are currently enduring a tough cycle.

I have hope and faith that this country can make it through this rough time in our nation's history. Right now, it might seem as though this deadly viral threat will never cease to end. Now I cannot state whether or not this epidemic will eventually fully subside, but with the Moderna, Pfizer, and Johnson & Johnson vaccines ready for distribution among the masses, an individual does have hope in life.

In this nation, we should understand how to navigate through life when change and life's cycle is challenging and difficult. This is a time in which the life cycle for the majority of individuals in our society is challenging and does not look promising. We all can overcome the negative cycles of life in spite of this ongoing pandemic.

Perception and perspective are key factors in how one views difficult trials and hardships. If one cannot perceive the trial as a means to improve and mature as an individual, then likely that individual will have a negative perspective of that situation. I am not saying that one should view the pandemic as something that is positive. What I do believe an individual can gain from enduring this pandemic is an appreciation for life.

Some do not have a zeal for life due to the spread of this deadly virus. It is easy to lose sight of how life will not always become a smooth transition. I am a firm believer that trials and difficulties help mold and shape an individual's moral character.

If an individual can survive becoming infected with the COVID-19 virus, then he or she should have a new perspective of life. Hopefully, a survivor of the virus will not be the same person. After battling and defeating an unprecedented infectious disease, an individual will be more readily receptive when life becomes difficult, tough, and unpredictable.

Although one might become better equipped to endure negative circumstances in life, it does not mean that the individual will automatically receive life's hardships positively with welcoming arms. One thing that every individual must take into consideration in the era of COVID-19 is the fact that this virus is totally preventable. If we know that becoming stricken with the disease can be avoided, then there is a glimmer of hope that the negative cycle of life, which we are presently in, could have the potential of a positive and meaningful outcome.

In life, all that an individual has is the ability to have a positive mindset despite what life may bring. When an individual survives a life-threatening virus, it is a positive achievement and accomplishment. It is something that could cause someone to become thankful for surviving a hardship in life that is overwhelming and not easy to overcome or combat.

This should offer some encouragement to those in the midst of the COVID-19 battle. It could have a positive effect on an individual when there is an example of someone overcoming a negative situation or circumstance. Once a mindset and attitude of confidence and optimism is established, then life will have a greater meaning.

I am fully aware that the COVID-19 viral pandemic has been an unpleasant surprise. This virus gained momentum in this nation, as well as worldwide, in a short instant. I truly believe that most people living in this era of COVID-19 could not have imagined how life would be affected by an invisible viral pestilence that would soon become a deadly worldly phenomenon.

Overcoming the COVID-19 virus can become a difficult and tedious process for many in the midst of the battle. Some battling the infectious disease will appreciate the relentless regimen if it will result in a second chance to live their life in the right way. Every living human should experience all of life's emotions. The COVID-19 virus will test an individual's ability to accept life from the good, the bad, and the ugly.

Every day that we live in the era of COVID-19 will hopefully bring us one step closer to a permanent cure for this virus. As individuals living during these times, it is imperative that we aspire to live each day with joy and anticipation. We must anticipate the day when the world and society can move past the negative circumstances of this horrendous epidemic.

Our world and society must continue to pick up the pieces from this viral threat. This is how life is, a series of adaptations and adjustments. Due to the COVID-19 virus, every individual in the world does not have the option to remain in the same mindset.

I believe that COVID-19 has influenced many to live each day as if it is one's last. Furthermore, one cannot focus on trivial matters in life. What is more important than insignificant things in this life is how one recovers from tragedy.

Recovering from any type of negative experience is never easy. Sometimes it might take years to develop a semblance of normalcy. In regard to the COVID-19 virus, life at this moment has not returned back to the way it was.

This new way of life in which we are living as a result of the viral outbreak is extremely foreign to many. Think about it. Some are unfriendly and on edge due to all the restrictions in our world and society. Although traveling to a distant country can still occur, as a result of COVID-19, many of the airlines which specialized in foreign travel are not as prominent as they were before the onset of this global pandemic.

Some are complaining about travel restrictions instead of focusing on how to stay healthy and well. Though traveling to a distant land is exciting as well as enjoyable, it is something in life that is often viewed as a form of pleasure. Right now, during this pandemic, most individuals have survival on their minds.

It seems as though we are currently living in a survival-of-the-fittest mode. In all of my forty-plus years, I could not have imagined how so many in this nation, as well as others worldwide, are broken because of this virus. This goes to show you how nothing in life is assured or remains the same.

One must realize how taking a daily approach to life could help someone gradually come out of one's brokenness. This will require both time and a new perspective on the hurt and pain of a difficult period in one's life. From a spiritual perspective, there are various reasons why God has allowed such pain and suffering, stemming from this infectious viral pestilence.

Could it be that the Creator is trying to get the attention of those who have abandoned Him? I believe that the heavenly Father can use tragic events and circumstances to reveal to the individuals who are experiencing tragedy that living each day for Him is the only way to live. Only the Almighty, Himself, can help one acquire the strength to experience trials, such as COVID-19.

Finding the good in this tragic circumstance can prove difficult. There is not anything positive about the loss of lives. From tragedy, I believe that something good and helpful could result from it.

For example, before this pandemic, many families did not spend a plethora of time together. Some parents of children pre-pandemic had limited interaction with them. It seemed that the only time a parent would be able to spend quality time with their child or children was in the mornings and late in the evening.

The COVID-19 virus has inadvertently helped some families come closer together. It also provided the opportunity for families to appreciate one another. With the spread of this virus, life must not be lived without someone you love.

I am cognizant of the fact that family can be annoying at times, especially when they are continuously in close proximity. With the uncertainty of life, I am certain that families would deal with an annoying family member or loved one. Personally, I would rather have someone whom I love annoy me at times if it means that they are able to avoid becoming stricken with the virus.

It is a good day in life when one can maintain their health and avoid another day of contracting COVID-19. As a result of the mass amount of people perishing from this illness, life is more valuable than ever. One must strive to have more good days rather than bad ones.

We all must accept that there will be bad days no matter what an individual does. In other words, days in which everything that could go wrong does go wrong has been an experience in which many have experienced one time or another. When it comes to COVID-19, many are dealing with the fact that it, too, is a negative experience that is inevitable and has the potential to become never-ending.

How would you feel if you suddenly became stricken with the COVID-19 virus? Most would take that news as if it were a bad dream. If you happen to contract COVID-19, try not to view it as an automatic death sentence. Perceiving the contraction of the COVID-19 virus from the perspective that illnesses and sicknesses are just a product of life can help the individual who is afflicted with the virus perceive it more favorably.

I am not saying that one should receive sickness without any hurt or disappointment, but perceiving it positively could lead to both a positive perspective and perception of it. When an individual accepts sickness as one of life's necessities, one will take each day that one has to combat an illness, such as COVID-19, in stride. This mindset is most desirable in the defeat of this dangerous disease.

In this era of COVID-19, life has not been joyous and positive. One must value one's life and health because this virus can negatively affect an individual without a moment's notice. Life right now is difficult no matter where you reside, but pressing through a viral pandemic and coming out on the positive side of it will make challenges such as COVID-19 worthwhile.

Storms in life will arise. The COVID-19 virus has become a continuous trial in this country, as well as all around the world. I believe that we do not have any choice but to endure the misfortune.

If you have faith, then you will know that storms and rainy seasons will pass. My hope is that the COVID-19 virus will eventually subside, and the nation along with the world can overcome and move on from it. We all collectively must become patient and weather this mishap.

As we progress in life, we will encounter situations that will test our courage and faith. COVID-19 has many questioning whether or not life is worth the challenge. I wholeheartedly believe in the recovery of an individual in regard to a negative event or circumstance.

Individuals with a positive and strong mindset are not allowing the threat of COVID-19 to influence them to have a negative opinion of life. This does not mean that the individual who is positive is not feeling the effect of this global phenomenon. Realistically, everyone who is walking on earth is experiencing the lingering effect in which this virus has caused.

What can you do in this COVID-19 virus storm? I believe that the only thing that one can do is face the storm. Storms in life can become scary and difficult, but they will not last forever. At the conclusion of the storm, the sun will shine.

COVID-19 has impacted every facet of life. If you can remain calm during this time of extreme difficulty, the heavenly Father will give you the strength and courage to endure this unprecedented trial called COVID-19. It is unbelievable how this virus has allowed many to lose hope that one day the virus will either become tamed or be a footnote in the history of infectious diseases.

Let's face it: storms can become deadly. The COVID-19 virus has proven that it is such. When storms on earth appear, no one can avoid them because they are inevitable.

Weather storms can formulate without any warning. Some storms make landfall and destroy homes and businesses. After the storm, the individuals who were affected by it cannot do anything else but recover and rebuild.

In regard to the COVID-19 virus, there is a rebuilding process that must take place. As a society, we have to rebuild our economy, as well as our collective fragile mental state. The rebuilding of our society is essential in the mind and hearts of many in this country and also worldwide.

Some might suggest that the COVID-19 virus would not have occurred if a certain country were not responsible for the outbreak of it. There is blame given by those who do not understand how this particular storm or trial God foreknew before anyone was ever created would occur. When storms arise, especially in the era of COVID-19, it is best to weather it.

Consistency in one's daily mood can elude some due to this uncontrollable outbreak. It requires a plethora of courage and prayer not to allow this pestilence to get you down. There will be times in life that sadness will appear in our lives.

With the continuous news coverage on this pandemic, I can understand why many do not have happiness and joy. It is difficult to experience any type of laughter in the times in which we live. If you are able to laugh about at least one thing within a given day, then mentally you are on the road to having a positive mental state.

We are to ultimately live out our days on this earth one day at a time. Yesterday is gone, and we cannot do anything about tomorrow. The only thing that one can do is live in the present tense.

As we live in the current state of our world and society, there is so much unhappiness and anxiety. Many are filled with these emotions due to the fear of this viral threat. I believe that these emotions are definitely valid.

There is a life-threatening infectious disease that is destroying the masses. Although this is an ongoing reality, one must strive to maintain a consistent mood. I suggest that one acquire a positive mood of consistency by focusing on one's faith and doing activities, which will keep one busy, while occupying one's mind.

The bottom line in regard to the COVID-19 virus is that it is now a significant fixture in our world and society. Instead of living in uncertainty and fear, one must strive to replace that mindset with optimism and hope. One has to develop the positive mindset that this virus will not always become detrimental to our society.

Tough times and circumstances are essential in life. If misfortune and trials do not occur, then how can one develop insight and character? Difficulties in life usually prepare those experiencing it to accept it as part of being human. This virus, though difficult to fathom, is already making an impact on the character of many individuals in this world and nation to cherish this brief life.

When we experience life exactly how it is supposed to happen, we are more likely not to panic. COVID-19, like it or not, was destined to happen. One cannot move forward without accepting that fact.

COVID-19 has essentially been a life-changing perilous experience. Some will fortunately become better, morally, after experiencing a potentially near-death experience. Life is not always about gloom and doom.

Successfully overcoming COVID-19 will motivate many to appreciate and become thankful for the life that they do have. No one really knows what life has in store for any individual. There could be a storm or a ray of sunshine awaiting someone. Whatever circumstances becomes the result of an individual facing the COVID-19 virus, viewing it as one of life's experiences is one of the keys to enduring and overcoming it.

CHAPTER 6

Hold on to Positive Memories

Right now it might seem that because of this pandemic, one cannot think about the joy and laughter of the past. Some say that we are to forget about the things that occurred previously. Personally, I beg to differ with those who suggest that one do not look from behind.

The COVID-19 virus has many reverting back to previous memories. Frankly, I do not blame an individual who is longing for happy thoughts and memories of yesteryear. Our world and nation is in the most turbulent and chaotic time in its history and existence.

I believe that positive memories of the past will help keep an individual sane. Also, good memories could result in hope. As we all are aware, hope is definitely needed in the era of the viral pandemic.

I have memories of unity in our country. There was a period in the 1990s that seemed as though people were coming together. During that decade, the United States was also prospering economically.

Though the decade of the 1990s had its fair share of negative events and occurrences overall, I can recall that decade as being the time in which transition from isolation of various groups manifested into inclusion. This was a time in which love and unity seemed prominent. It also seemed during that decade, our nation was not as divided as it is today.

In the 1990s, I was primarily a student. I spent the early years of that decade in high school, and the latter part of that decade in college. Most of the memories I enjoyed during that time were fun activities. Going to social functions, concerts, parks, and sports events without worrying about life-threatening situations, such as terrorism and the COVID-19 virus, was simple and fun. Now it is difficult to enjoy those events without the slightest hint of anxiety.

The news coverage during those years had its share of negative stories, but I can also recall how there were positive and motivating stories that flooded the airwaves. Now every newscast is talking about the uncontrollable amount of deaths stemming from this viral epidemic. When all one hears on one's radio and television is the increasing number of deaths by the masses, it is understandable how one's memories can play a vital role.

A youth growing up in the era of the COVID-19 pandemic might not be as fortunate as those who are mature and seasoned in the development of fun memories in their lives. I feel deep sympathy for individuals who are attending school, especially in these times that we are in. Fun activities, in which many individuals who are young and vibrant might enjoy, are now mainly prohibited.

I am not saying that a young individual growing up today does not have any fun memories or activities to rely upon. We all have some kind of fun memory of the past. An individual living during this global viral outbreak should not shun positive and enjoyable memories which can improve one's attitude and mood in these chaotic times. In the COVID-19 battle, memories are just as crucial as a potential cure.

Memories of hope will sustain any individual experiencing a difficult time. It is beneficial to one's mind to have hopeful thoughts. Without these thoughts, the mind will only replay memories of negativity and pessimism.

Some who are living in the COVID-19 pandemic era only have short memories of hope. As a nation, this is not the first or last epidemic that will wreak havoc. This country has been blessed in previous years by coming up with cures and remedies for diseases and illnesses that were once deemed incurable.

In the meanwhile, one must rely upon pleasant memories to get one through the day. One should not be preoccupied with the staggering death toll of people perishing from COVID-19. Instead, train your mind to formulate a compilation of sweet memories.

If you are married or in a relationship, then revert back to the first time that you met your significant other. Typically, memories of love relationships will provide the memory to briefly escape all the negative occurrences which could cloud the mind. Suppose a significant other is not the memory that you prefer to think about.

There are other memorable occurrences in an individual's life that are enjoyable and pleasant. For example, one could recollect a past accomplishment or achievement. Sometimes memories of accomplishments can give an individual newfound confidence and hope.

Hope and confidence are needed each day. As a community and a nation, we have to collectively hold on to memories that bring us hope for the future. Sure, there are some memories which threaten happy and pleasant ones.

I am certain that no one will have pleasant memories of COVID-19. This is why it is imperative to reflect upon memories of joy and peace. Realistically, one cannot always remain in a state of recollection.

It is unhealthy to solely rely upon memory alone. We have to strive to always create new memories of happiness. There are health conditions which can formulate when the mind and brain is always fixated on a previous time or experience.

The goal for any individual living in these unprecedented times is to strive to remain hopeful and optimistic. I am cognizant about how the events and occurrences in our world and society are not providing a positive snapshot. In order to remain in an optimistic mindset, I believe that it is okay to reminisce about pleasant memories from time to time.

A pleasant memory is difficult to maintain in the negative times in which we currently live. The COVID-19 virus has forced many to reflect to the time when life was not filled with utter chaos. Memories of love, joy, and peace are what many living during these turbulent times should strive to obtain. Past memories are welcomed in order to face the reality of this debilitating viral enemy.

Imagine becoming stricken with COVID-19. Initially, one will experience a plethora of emotions. The most prominent emotion that one might have is fear.

COVID-19 is a virus like no other. Part of the process of combating the disease is the patient experiencing mandatory isolation. When an individual is isolated, he or she is left to one's own imagination and thoughts.

If you happen to become infected with the COVID-19 virus, it really does matter if you can recall positive memories. While isolated, assuming that one has a severe case of the virus, the infected individual will typically become hospitalized. Once in the confines of the hospital, a COVID-19 patient will spend the majority of their time in a hospital room by oneself.

Although I have been fortunate enough to avoid becoming stricken with COVID-19, I can definitely empathize with an individual struggling with the disease. It is difficult as well as a great feat to battle a virus that takes a toll on one's physical and mental health. An individual who unfortunately contracts COVID-19 essentially battles the illness not only externally but also internally.

The COVID-19 virus, I can imagine, will weigh heavily on an individual's psyche. A mind filled with positive memories of triumph is needed in order to overcome the illness. I believe that the individual who is battle-tested mentally can retract past victories of overcoming an illness or disease.

We all have the ability to overcome anything in life with the right mentality. It is difficult for an individual in the midst of a COVID-19 battle to recall positive memories, while experiencing the physical effects of the illness along with feelings of loneliness. Though I am not a mental health professional, I believe that an individual experiencing the virus, while in the hospital, should have a relationship with some type of licensed expert on psychological conditions.

Now I am not saying that the individual who has contracted COVID-19 is automatically mentally challenged, but I wholeheartedly believe that an expert on mental health can become one of the catalysts for recovery. With the isolation as a result of this viral threat, an individual who is in tune with oneself, cognitively and psychologically, could become equipped with the tools from a health expert to mentally recall memories of overcoming or overachieving in something.

Coping with the COVID-19 virus can become a challenging-and-difficult task. Each individual who is hospitalized from the disease does not have the support of family and loved ones physically. The only method in which a COVID-19 patient can rely upon is retention.

This virus is a battle over one's survival. Although the isolation from the illness can result in an individual becoming lonesome, that individual really is not. Intense thoughts of positive memories are there for an individual to fill the mind and brain with joy and comfort.

Some suggest that laughter is good medicine. I agree that it (laughter) can positively affect an individual's mood and outlook. In the midst of battling the COVID-19 virus, laughter can elude many.

One might think to oneself that we are living in serious and perilous times, and there is not any need to laugh. This virus has threatened the basics of life, like enjoying a laughable joke or memory. As a world and society, we are bombarded with a plethora of important issues that will have an enormous effect.

Every individual living in the era of the COVID-19 pandemic must set aside time to take their daily dose of medicine. You might be saying inwardly that you do not partake in putting any kind of drugs in your body. The medicine in which I am referring to is those laughable memories.

Our world and society is in utter chaos and turmoil. When I am able to venture out in public, I can feel the intensity of tension in the air. No longer do I hear laughter among individuals in public places.

Personally, I can understand why some people are not taking their daily dose of laughter. Laughter and good memories of the past have been replaced with worry and anxiety. There are many who feel that there is not any point in laughter when you factor in what is taking place in our society, besides the pandemic.

Everyone has some semblance of a good memory in one's life. I believe that many cannot survive or thrive in life without positive memories. It does not matter whether one's good memories of the past are vast or minute; identifying these memories can help an individual not to become so frustrated with life.

Individuals with a mindset of frustration are in deep need of an outlet. Having good memories of laughter, peace, and hope will help the individual temporarily escape the life-altering and life-threatening issue of the ongoing viral pandemic. As human beings, we grow and evolve when we are not in a position of stagnation.

Sure, it is not always easy to become receptive to experience life when our routines and daily regimens are subject to change. COVID-19 has single-handedly altered the lives of many who were content in life before this viral outbreak. Instead of choosing to take one's medicine of laughter and good memories, a plethora of individuals have abandoned the option of remaining positive during a difficult time.

One might think that there is no way that laughter can have an impact in one's life, especially in an unprecedented viral pandemic. In my opinion, an individual can find humor even in the midst of chaos. While we are in this adversity and challenge, try to find something to laugh about.

In our minds, we all have the ability and option to fill it with good and positive memories, or inject it with thoughts of anxiety and frustration. We all have a choice. Do not allow this viral disease epidemic to alter your laughable thoughts.

Experience is considered a great teacher. The COVID-19 virus has taught us that it is imperative for an individual to create some type of positive memory from an unbelievable situation. We all have gained experience on how to conduct ourselves in the midst of a viral outbreak.

Though the COVID-19 virus is a negative circumstance, I believe a positive memory of survival and victory can be formulated when an individual is fortunate to overcome this negative ordeal. Sometimes positive memories will come from a negative situation. Once an individual is able to defeat and recover from COVID-19, that person will always be able to lean on the memory of that experience.

Healing from any type of illness or sickness can become vigorous. Also, one will develop a newfound energy and perspective on battling illnesses. A positive perception stems from a collection of thoughts, which can be greatly affected by a simple memory.

While the world as a whole is experiencing negativity due to this global pandemic, one can recall how they were able to come out on the right side of difficulties. Recalling past misfortunes is beneficial in overcoming trials. COVID-19 is a unique trial because it is hugely widespread.

Some might desire to avoid all memories of trials and difficulties. In some instances, the negative experiences, which were eventually overcome, are mentally blocked. One reason why a difficult experience is not in the memory of an individual is because the experience is too painful to recall.

There are many who would like to forget about the year that the COVID-19 virus became prevalent among the masses. Since this pandemic appeared, the world and society cannot forget how devastating and detrimental this virus is. Hopefully if the COVID-19 virus is able to stop spreading, some will ultimately have the option of recalling a hurtful and painful memory in our world.

As a culture and society, we have always remembered significant and painful events. Through the recollection of pain, an individual can help others heal. I believe that recalling negative and tragic events with others, such as the COVID-19 virus, will help the individual(s) better process the situation.

Memories of events and tragedy affects a variety of people in various ways. The one thing that everyone will agree upon is the onset of how the COVID-19 virus has literally changed how we interact with people. Currently we have memories of how it was like to hug someone without worrying about if the individual is contagious or not. We have become a world and society that is increasingly becoming more socially distant. Because we are a world and nation in the midst of a highly contagious infectious disease, no one can blame many for emphasizing space and distance, and due to this, one must have clear and positive memories. Living in the COVID-19 era has challenged all who are living in it to cherish special moments.

Nostalgia is what many living through this pandemic will experience. In reality, our world might not return to any semblance of peace until the Second Coming. In my opinion, the COVID-19 virus has forced many to become sentimental.

I was once a critic of technology. But now, due to the limitations that the COVID-19 virus has influenced upon our society, I must say that I am an advocate of the technological world. There is not too much that one can do in regard to venturing out and about in public.

We only can take so much of negative television within a day. The only other thing that one can do is turn on the computer. I only suggest that one turn on one's personal computer when there is nothing left to do.

The computer has been a reliable source of history and nostalgia. One can go on the Internet or YouTube to view one's favorite videos of the past. Before the outbreak of this pandemic, there were many who were searching the web on various nostalgic videos.

Since the spread of this epidemic, views on videos and YouTube have astronomically increased. Of course, it does not take a genius to know why these views on YouTube have widely gained more popularity. There are many who would prefer to watch videos of nostalgia to help them to remember how life was during a specific period in time.

No individual desires to view the continuous headlines on the spread of the COVID-19 virus. Watching videos on YouTube of past videos can get an individual's mind and mood in order. I believe that it is healthy mentally when an individual can revert back to past history that made one feel happy and positive.

Sometimes an old picture or video can instantly take one back to a happy period in one's life. Viewing high school and college yearbooks can place that individual back to that point in time. With the occurrence of this pandemic, we all need to view pictures and videos which will spark pleasant and positive memories.

Though we cannot do anything about the past, positive memories of nostalgia can do more good than harm. If you are a sports fan, many of the sports stations thrive on nostalgic plays and games. Fans, whose teams were better in the past than they are currently, can still have hope that their favorite team will eventually return to a time of past glory.

This could put the long-suffering sports fan in a more positive mood. I understand that the stakes are much higher for each individual living in the era of COVID-19, more than a sports game which is typically viewed as entertainment. Pictures and videos, on the other hand, could bring hope and joy to the individual in the midst of this pandemic.

History is always an indication of how far we have come. Memories also reveals one's history. One must rely upon one's nostalgic memories to help them cope with COVID-19. Although many will have unpleasant memories of the COVID-19 virus, hopefully positive and pleasant memories will continue to have dominion over one's mind.

Trials and difficulties can become overwhelming. We are enduring an unprecedented mishap, which no one in our lifetime has ever experienced. If you are a God-fearing individual, then you are aware that there are some difficulties in life that only He can solve.

I believe that it is imperative that we recall past situations that resulted in victory. The United States as a whole has been blessed to experience past success in regard to solving medical challenges. In the early twentieth century, there were illnesses—such as, the Spanish Flu, polio, and the measles—that threatened the citizens of our country.

Sure, these illnesses plagued many in our society during that time, and by the grace of the Creator and competent medical experts, vaccines were created. As I am writing this book, there is a potential vaccine, made by the Pfizer drug company, which offers hope to those who might be infected with the COVID-19 virus in the future. If this drug, which has reported to be 90%–95% effective in the preliminary process, does help diminish the spread of COVID-19, it will invoke memories of past treatments that were effective in a widespread epidemic.

Each individual living in the COVID-19 era must hold on to positive memories of combating and defeating a trial in life. When an individual is in the midst of a trial or battle, that individual might not view their situation as having the potential for a positive memory. Yes, the COVID-19 virus has created division among many in this nation, but I believe that there is some in our society who have gained an increasing amount of respect for family.

Although this virus is the prime example of destruction and negativity, it has also brought some families together. Sometimes negative circumstances can yield to positive outcomes. This trial of the COVID-19 virus has created fond memories for loved ones to recall the time in which they were able to go from estranged to having a prominent role in each other's lives again.

God, Himself, can do the impossible. He can take a worldwide pandemic and reveal to health experts the specific treatment for an uncontrollable viral outbreak. There is cause for optimism in our world and society. Hopefully, in the near future, the threat of someone perishing from COVID-19 will not be as detrimental as it was previously.

One thing we all should do in our world and society is always remember and acknowledge God, who brought you out of the trial. The COVID-19 virus has had both positive and, of course, negative effects all around the world. Because of all the negativity in which many are experiencing due to this pandemic, positive memories could become difficult to obtain. My hope is that families create positive memories of love and unity in spite of the negative circumstances of this virus. If we as a world and society are able to overcome a widespread infectious disease, then the positive memory of defeating and becoming victorious over it should be embedded in one's positive memory bank.

Love will bring any individual through a turbulent crisis. There has been so much talk about the COVID-19 virus that the subject of love has essentially taken a backseat. If an individual cannot recall the love from a spouse or significant other, then how can that individual endure a life-threatening virus? I wholeheartedly believe that love has helped some individuals who were afflicted with COVID-19, a chance to survive the disease.

From my understanding of an individual who is experiencing a severe bout with the COVID-19 virus, that infected person will have minimal contact at best with a spouse or loved one. An individual who can hold on to the love that is demonstrated by a loving husband or wife will fight to make it back to them. Loving memories of a spouse or significant other is synonymous with memories of love and optimism.

We all have relationships. Not only does one have kinship with a spouse or a relationship with a significant other, but one also can form a strong one with friends as well as other family members. Individuals who have a close relationship with another individual will have positive and loving memories of that person. Typically, memories of love can stand the test of time.

Some do not have the luxury of having a relative or spouse always in close proximity. That individual who does not have family nearby might have to travel for work. Although traveling is a requirement for some, I am certain that the individual is cognizant of the fact that they are loved.

When an individual is battling a disease that requires isolation in order to heal, memories of love must be at the forefront of one's mind. Having loving memories of a family could help any individual encounter any trial or challenge that might seem insurmountable to overcome. There is a sense of security when an individual can reflect back to a past or current memory in which a loving comment was exchanged.

One who has an array of loving memories embedded in one's mind does not have to worry or have anxiety about the challenges that some will encounter after battling the COVID-19 virus. Knowing that someone is there for them can make a significant difference between defeating and combating this viral threat. I am not suggesting that every individual who has loving memories and a supportive family will be able to become victorious over this disease consistently.

Due to the will of the Creator, loving memories alone will not be able to determine whether or not an individual will survive this terrible trial and ordeal. Unfortunately, perishing from the COVID-19 virus is a terrifying reality in our world. Memories of friends and loved ones can give an individual the strength and courage to battle this epidemic.

An individual who is battling the COVID-19 virus will need every memory of good times, especially if one is battling the disease in the ICU unit in a hospital. Sadly, one who unfortunately is stricken with the illness does not have the warmth of a gentle touch from those who are closest to them. No matter what becomes the fate of an individual who has contracted this dangerous virus, loving memories of hope and love must always become one's internal focus.

Positive memories will sustain those who might be battling this horrendous virus. It is imperative to reflect during these uncertain times in order to continue in mental wellness. In some instances, the only thing in which one can rely upon is pleasant memories from the past.

I personally think of victorious and triumphant times in our nation. When I think of those days of prosperity in our country, it brings me back to happier times. Hopefully a reliable vaccine will help with the dark mood of many in our world and society.

We as a nation have usually overcome medical dilemmas. After many of the health issues of concern subsided, our country has been able to bounce back. My hope for this nation, as well as other nations worldwide, is for all its citizens to be able to collectively experience happiness and joy again.

This viral pandemic has turned many smiles upside down. Remembering those days of laughter and joy can help alleviate a mood of deep sadness. Some are not fortunate to move on from those negative feelings and emotions.

One must continue to develop some form of a positive memory, although there is not much to become happy about. It is a blessing when an individual can experience another birthday. There are always memories in which one can formulate in this era of the viral pandemic.

Spending time with family members and loved ones while making another birthday will create new positive memories. I am aware that due to the COVID-19 virus, one will not be able to celebrate their birthday in the same way that one did in previous years. One cannot safely celebrate it with a plethora of people around.

These are the times in which we all must adapt. For some, adapting to change is quite difficult to adjust to. If one could recall how they were able to adapt to past difficulties, then one will be able to have a more positive experience in spite of hardship.

Dealing with the COVID-19 virus on a daily basis for these last several months has challenged the way in which we think and process our thoughts. Living through this global epidemic is tough on the mental mindset of an individual. For many, there is not any time to have reflection about how things were before this viral outbreak.

When an individual is in a life-and-death struggle, it is difficult to formulate thoughts of pleasantness and joy. Now I do not profess to know what it is like to experience the COVID-19 viral battle, but I can only empathize and imagine how helpless an individual affected severely by this virus must feel. A COVID-19 patient is, sadly, not only at the mercy of the doctors and medical staff who care and spend time with them, but the infected individual could also be a casualty of one's mind and thoughts.

I believe that one must always have hope regardless of what is happening around them. Previous memories of the past, especially if it embodies overcoming a struggle, are crucial in successfully living through this unprecedented pandemic. It is human nature to repeat behaviors in which one is accustomed to. If you can recall acting in courage in the past, that memory will serve one well during this pestilence.

Mental recognition of memories of trials can either produce mental awareness or instability. Unfortunately, there are a plethora of individuals who are succumbing to the mental stress that this pandemic has caused. One must be thankful that they have the mental fortitude to recall overcoming previous misfortunes.

There is not anything wrong with recalling difficult times. When we are able to reflect upon memories of struggle, the memories will not only help one learn from the experience but insight and mental growth will usually become the result. If an individual living and surviving through this pandemic is fortunate to have reflection from their experience with either contracting the virus or living in the COVID-19 era, he or she will be able to have memories of courage and strength.

Living in the COVID-19 era requires a plethora of patience and endurance. One has to persevere not only physically but mentally as well. We all have encountered previous situations in our lives in which patience and perseverance was required.

Relying upon those memories of endurance will become beneficial to the individual navigating through this uncertain era in life. An individual who can recall in their mind how a battle was endured can use that recollection of an experience to help them have perseverance in the COVID-19 battle. I suggest that one have at least one positive memory of endurance once a day.

These mental memories of reflection have a purpose during these difficult times. No one can endure a tough experience in life without accepting it as an inevitable occurrence. Experiencing the COVID-19 virus for many has been a memory in life, which will become difficult to avoid and forget.

In my opinion, the COVID-19 virus might not be the only life-threatening pestilence that we all will have to deal with in the future. Although we do not like what these disease epidemics brings to our world and society, it is important that we reflect back to how we handled ourselves in previous medical misfortunes. One's recollection of a negative circumstance, such as the COVID-19 virus, could be the difference between calmness and worry.

The state in which our present world and society is in due to this global pandemic is extremely disheartening. There are many who cannot come to terms with how our world has deteriorated. One must not allow their mind to also plunge in that state.

Personally, I believe that a positive memory commences and ends with one's optimism and perception of life. Presently, life has not been able to become enjoyed by many due to the ongoing threat of this invisible enemy. I am aware of how many of us do not have a plethora of special memories during these times of extreme difficulty.

Mental pictures of hope and courage will help an individual reflect upon positive images of the past. Positive memories can help the individual overcome negative moods of despair. One must never relinquish one's positive memories, although there is not much to positively recall at this time.

CHAPTER 7

One Day, There Will Be No More Viral Pandemic

Can you imagine not having to deal with a viral pandemic? This may not happen in this lifetime, but it will occur. We are living in the last days, and the earth as you know it will one day become vastly different. I am unqualified to state how our world will be when the Savior and Redeemer rules on earth, but I can say for certain that the COVID-19 virus and other diseases will not inflict harm on others during that time.

As a society, we must anticipate the day in which pestilences, such as COVID-19, will disappear. Sickness and diseases are an unfortunate reality which affects everyone. Many of us have personally encountered illnesses in our lives, or we have had family members experience some type of sickness.

While we are living on this present earth, we cannot avoid sickness. It is all around us. The COVID-19 virus has revealed to the masses that no matter how healthy you are, you can still become stricken with some type of sickness or disease.

Is COVID-19 going to be prevalent in our world in the future? Well I do not know the answer to that question for certain. In our current world, there might always be cases of the virus. In regard to the new heaven and earth that will form, I can confidently state that diseases will never again wreak havoc.

Although COVID-19 is a virus that is causing many to struggle in a variety of ways, one must view pestilences and diseases as temporal. Our time on this present earth is brief, no matter if you live past a hundred years of age. The COVID-19 virus has demonstrated that no one is assured of a long life.

Until the day that diseases and pestilences subside, each individual living in the era of COVID-19 should adapt the mantra that "life is brief." With a plethora of people each day perishing at an alarming rate, it is impossible not to see how it is becoming increasingly rare for an individual to experience those golden years. It is imperative that an individual living in these times of pestilences and diseases live a life of optimism and anticipation.

One day, the COVID-19 viral pandemic could become a non-factor in our present world. An individual must never lose hope and optimism that this mysterious virus can be tamed and controlled. Companies which specialize in vaccines have been working around the clock to come up with the solution to this difficult chapter in human existence.

If the current vaccines, which are currently available on the market, consistently exhibit promise in regard to this viral disease, it will essentially do wonders for the mood and morale of many in our world and society. Each individual who becomes infected with the virus can anticipate the day when the symptoms of the disease will no longer become a cause for concern because a vaccine is on the market. As a society, we must exhibit patience and also trust the process.

Previously, I discussed how there are currently at least three vaccines which are ready to combat this invisible threat. Though there are side effects from these potential treatments, hopefully it will serve its purpose and provide relief to a society and world that is filled with turmoil and chaos. In the coming weeks and months, we all will discover how these vaccines have fared.

Foreseeing a day without discussions of the COVID-19 virus will take some time to get used to. I can recall other life-threatening diseases and pestilences in our lifetime, which I thought would never dissolve in the daily news. COVID-19 is currently a deadly threat to all humanity, but I firmly believe that this virus has prepared many to seek out another alternative.

The alternative in which I am referring to is a heavenly one. I believe that this virus alone has caused some to consider the fact that they are not in control of one's life. Do not get me wrong: we do have freewill to make either wise or unwise choices in life.

We have a choice to follow rules and guidelines required by law and authority. There is another authoritative figure(s) who will make a difference in the life of an individual who might become uncertain about how to move forward in a positive manner while in the midst of continuous death. I am referring to the Creator and His Son, Jesus Christ.

When an individual is grounded in their spiritual walk with God, he or she can anticipate vividly the day in which pain, disease, and discomfort will no longer rule on earth. Though this virus is an enormous threat, the heavenly Father is greater than an epidemic. In our world and culture, we tend to focus on the immediate problem or issue.

Now I am not saying that we should not become focused on the issue of the COVID-19 pandemic because it is an extremely vital issue. Millions around the world, as well as millions in the United States, are affected by the continual threat of COVID-19. What I am saying is that focusing on the Creator in these difficult times will give an individual a heavenly perspective.

If you only have a worldly viewpoint of the COVID-19 virus, then this illness will negatively affect you physically, mentally, and spiritually. An individual who is worldly cannot envision a time when the health of individuals who have either perished or became severely infected with the virus will become restored at the arrival of the Messiah. Those who are also worldly will tend to focus on the utter chaos and destruction in the world instead of anticipating a future time of peace and harmony.

There is always hope and optimism which one can gather from drastic events and occurrences. One must become cognizant of the fact that this world is not all that there is. I understand how some cannot let go of the many enticements that it (the world) has to offer.

Everlasting hope is the result of those who have chosen the heavenly alternative. One must never downplay the importance of a spiritual guide during this deadly and unpredictable time in our world. I can confidently state that a relationship with the Creator and His Son is both beneficial and vital in the midst of this perilous pandemic.

Individuals who have hope for the future kingdom of heaven on earth are not fearful of the viral pandemic itself. These particular people place their hope in the Almighty and the Blessed Savior. Due to one's expectation that God is in control, even in the midst of utter destruction and turmoil, those who place their faith in Him are mindful of the fact that this disease epidemic is limited.

Imagine how the world would be if diseases and illnesses would not exist. It would be filled with individuals with strong and healthy bodies. Also, there would not have any type of worry and anxiety stemming from receiving devastating news of an incurable illness or disease, because the world would be void of sickness.

Health is a vital part of living a full-and-quality life. If an individual does not have at least satisfactory health, then he or she cannot experience a sufficient amount of joy and happiness. I am aware that there is a few instances of individuals with life-threatening illnesses who refused to allow their circumstances affect their life's duration.

COVID-19, thus far, has been considered among the top three causes of death currently in America. This is quite disturbing that an illness can affect a society with so much death. If the world in which we live is one day free from the COVID-19 virus, there will be millions who would not know how to react to such good news.

As a society, we must consider the fact that we all have a great chance of contracting COVID-19. It does not matter where or how you live, a disease such as COVID-19 could still appear out of nowhere. Recently I heard some individuals discussing what they would do when the virus is no longer a threat to society.

Some who were imagining life without COVID-19 think that life will resume back to normal. I do not profess to know how life could ever be experienced in the way that it was. There is a plethora of messes which our nation and world would have to clean up as a result of this pandemic.

For example, the economy and the current recession that we as a nation are now a part of would have to recover significantly. Since the onset of the pandemic, many restaurants and clothing stores have closed. It is amazing how an invisible virus can affect so many businesses and institutions.

One can only hope for the day that COVID-19 will become obsolete. Will it occur sooner rather than later? I believe that it remains to be seen. In the meantime, one should not be pessimistic while waiting for an answer in solving this mysterious virus.

Spiritually speaking, the COVID-19 virus is only a sample of what is soon to come to our world. No one could have prepared for an invisible threat that would alter the lives of billions of people. A positive way of viewing the COVID-19 virus and other future catastrophic events is that it has only a limited time to affect our world, as well as those who are stricken with it.

You must adopt the mindset of this viral epidemic becoming limited in our world in order to deal with the destruction and devastation that the illness has caused. Think about how life would be when this pandemic is over. It might seem that there is not any chance of the virus subsiding, but I am confident that one day it will. As of now, we all do not have any choice but to demonstrate patience and optimism.

How are we to continue to hold out hope that COVID-19 will not be detrimental to our world in the future? One way in which hope can be sustained is by knowing that this current earth is not our permanent home. Many perish in this life without realizing that this earth will be transformed. It will transition into a new earth which will not include the problems and issues that are prevalent on this present earth.

The COVID-19 virus might become a permanent fixture on this present earth if the vaccines that were produced are not dependable or reliable. Some cannot fathom the fact that pestilences will continue to harm many until the end of the age. An individual should accept the fact that COVID-19 might be curable one day in the near future, but there are others who remain skeptical.

Personally, I can envision the day that COVID-19 and other similar viruses will no longer harm innocent men, women, and children. I believe that hope will prevail in the midst of this negative circumstance. One should always anticipate relief from earthly chaos.

An individual might perish from the COVID-19 virus, but in their time of fighting the severe battle with the disease, the afflicted individual will discover peace when one eagerly anticipates being with the Creator and Savior. Now is the time to rely upon the heavenly Father for answers to life's difficulties. Having a personal relationship with Jesus is the key to having hope for a life that is free from the onset of the virus.

As mere humans, we are incapable of having anticipation of a better outcome without including the Savior in our lives. There are many who are more concerned with contracting the COVID-19 virus rather than God, who is able to provide the right mindset to the individual affected with the illness. In other words, one can have faith no matter what one's outcome might be.

There are very few people who can honestly maintain faith if they are able to defeat the disease, or who are unfortunately unable to overcome it. An individual can have faith while experiencing the severe effects of the COVID-19 virus. One will have the assurance of faith when one is cognizant of God's presence.

COVID-19 is a scary and mysterious illness. When an individual is aware that the pestilence will not have a negative effect in the eventual earth, one will soon be able to view the disease as ineffective in the future. As long as this present earth is existing, pestilences will affect it.

No one can decide what illnesses or diseases will become harmful. Initially, the COVID-19 virus was viewed as a non-threat when it first appeared on U.S. soil. This virus developed into a perilous pandemic in only a matter of weeks, which goes to show you how life can be changed and affected with a blink of an eye.

While we have life on earth, do not be surprised about how illnesses and diseases could be damaging one day, then on another day, it will not have any effect. What matters the most in regard to diseases and pestilences is one's overall perspective and perception. If you perceive the pestilence as one day becoming nonexistent, then it will ultimately give you the confidence to battle it.

The world in which we live has been declining before the onset of the COVID-19 virus. As members of this earth, a realistic but positive mindset must be at the core of each individual. Though no one is qualified to predict each future catastrophic occurrence, one must anticipate brighter days.

At this moment, it might seem as though the COVID-19 virus is having its way with the world. With the astronomical numbers of individuals perishing from the disease, it is quite difficult to dispute that fact. I am aware of how challenging it is to anticipate a world that is void of COVID-19.

From the beginning of time, diseases and plagues in our world and society have been prevalent. Our heavenly Father has blessed human beings with knowledge and intelligence. Fortunately, we have been able to overcome a plethora of diseases and illnesses that was, for a time, thought to be too difficult to recover from.

It has become an unforeseen goal for the ceasing of this deadly virus. Some are hopeful that one day this viral outbreak will not become a cause for caution and concern. There will be a day in the future in which person-to-person contact will not become a deadly health risk.

I do not know if our world and society will ever return to the days in which a touch, hug, or a kiss is not potentially life-threatening. This virus can either mysteriously disappear in the same way in which it appeared or remain prominent. Thus far, there is cautious optimism that COVID-19, though lethal in severe cases, can be defeated.

As a society, we are at the mercy of the health scientists and experts in regard to returning to the day that individuals are not on edge due to this pandemic. The key component of solving the mystery of the COVID-19 virus is time. Victims of this viral foe might become hopeless if these vaccines are not potent treatments in the prolonging of one's life.

Those who are battling the virus with all their might must continue to have optimism that their fight is not in vain. If scientists can eventually solve the origin of this infectious disease, then less people will not perish from COVID-19. Once this is established, our world and society could become less chaotic and toxic.

It might be wishful thinking to have optimism that our world can become less destructive if this viral infectious disease is solved. I believe that as long as you are a living and breathing human being, then it is always beneficial to one's mind and heart to have a glimmer of hope. One should not allow sickness and disease to alter one's future expectations.

Although the world that we reside in is increasingly becoming more turbulent, we must always hope for a better future. The threat of COVID-19 will eventually subside. It might not diminish hastily or at a rapid pace, but I know that if the issue of this potentially deadly pestilence is not resolved completely, the frustrations of many will become even more prevalent. Hopefully this viral epidemic will become less of a factor sooner rather than later.

There will be a coming time in which the threat of COVID-19 will not have any influence in life. One might have reservations that this will occur. Some cannot imagine having a society that is virally free.

In the present world, the COVID-19 virus is dominant. An individual cannot go one day without hearing about how this disease has resulted in numerous deaths. Due to the enormous amount of individuals perishing from this disease, some have not received a proper burial.

When this outbreak initially occurred, I did not envision how it would end or cease. Day after day, I would view the news in cities such as New York and Los Angeles, and I must admit that my hope for this viral pandemic becoming obsolete one day had wavered. Realistically, the virus may not cease to end in this fallen world.

This reminds me of other health crises which were thought of as uncontrollable but was eventually controlled. The illness or disease might still affect some in society, but when a vaccine was developed for that particular ailment, the illness did not negatively affect society in the same way. My hope is that COVID-19 will soon be in the same category as illnesses and diseases which invoked fear initially then eventually became less threatening to the masses.

COVID-19 will not affect this nation in the future when its citizens are able to fully recover. This is not to say that there will never again have cases of the COVID-19 virus. No more COVID-19 means that it will not cause any widespread destruction or devastating trauma.

Each passing day, we are coming closer to solving the spread of this virus. As a society, it will be a glorious time when the threat of this invisible enemy does not endanger every member of it. What is intriguing about this virus is the fact that it does not take much for it to spread.

The air that we breathe cannot be enjoyed due to the threat of this viral pestilence. My hope is that the virus will not continue to become easily contractible. Sure, we know that the virus can be contracted, though the individual is trying one's best to follow all the precautions and guidelines that are suggested.

Living in the era of the COVID-19 pandemic requires a great deal of poise and optimism. On one hand, it serves no purpose to allow this viral threat to steal your hope and optimism in future endeavors, but also I can see how agonizing dealing with an illness like COVID-19 could become. Our future and hope depends upon how well we are able to cope with change, as well as less-than-ideal circumstances.

It is easy to take one's eyes off the prize when trials and difficulties seem overwhelming and less likely to happen. In regard to the viral infectious disease epidemic diminishing, this too might seem unattainable. When people can pray and have faith that the virus will be tamed, the prize of having a healthy life can and will be obtained and accomplished.

Staying optimistic and positive under the predicament that our nation and world is in is challenging to say the least. Optimism in the midst of a growing pandemic is not easy for some. Recently there have been significant studies in the war against the COVID-19 viral epidemic.

In the news headlines, it has been reported that there are more vaccines in development to combat the spread of the COVID-19, which could prove to be effective. With these vaccines that could potentially stop the spread of the virus dead in its tracks, there is a sense of optimism in an otherwise dreadful reality. Though there are positive signs in some instances in regard to this terrible pandemic, still some remain unconvinced how we can all avoid becoming affected by this devastating disease.

The only thing that I can suggest to the millions living and affected by COVID-19 is to welcome the fact that a well-deserved break from this viral enemy is potentially on the horizon. While many around the world are embracing for more trials due to the COVID-19 virus, you could inwardly anticipate how this virus might not always become the detriment to millions in our society. No one deserves to be afflicted by this deadly and unpredictable illness.

There is a long and, at times, lonely road in the quest to defeat COVID-19. Just like in any other difficult battle in life, combating and having mastery over this virus does not always occur immediately. I know that in the United States, many of its citizens are not accustomed to waiting and having patience.

If illnesses and diseases of the magnitude of COVID-19 were immediately resolved, then there would not be any need for hope and anticipation. Also, the lives of many would not be in an enormous amount of jeopardy. Well this scenario would only play out in a nearly perfect world.

We all know that the world and society in which we live will never be able to produce perfection. This is why there is always a threat of pestilences and diseases such as the COVID-19 virus. In other words, sickness and disease are typically a necessary evil which must be endured by every living human.

As our world and society anticipates the dominance of the COVID-19 virus tapering off, each individual living during the time of this viral pandemic must not forget how they were able to survive this misfortune. Although one can never become complacent, it is always satisfying when turmoil and utter destruction are in the rearview mirror. Sometimes in life, pain and heartache are difficult to experience, but in the end, an unwelcome hurt can yield to a positive and mature mindset.

Are you anticipating the day that this global pandemic and epidemic will no longer threaten you, your friends, and loved ones? If you are staying positive in spite of these current circumstances, then do not stop. Try to uplift your spirit by remembering a breakthrough in previous hopeless situations.

Until the day that COVID-19 becomes a footnote in our history, in regard to life-threatening illnesses, take time to treasure each waking moment. In my opinion, we have lost the very essence of what it is to live life one day at a time. There are a plethora of emotions in which one could experience within a given day, but the greatest emotion that one could bestow upon another individual is love.

When I view the lack of empathy of some who have suddenly become familiar with death, I question that individual's empathy and love for the victim who has succumbed to the virus. The individuals with whom I am referring to are the nurses and medical staff who are caring for the COVID-19 patient. Sadly, some working in the chaos of hospitals are now immune to the thousands of patients who will typically, in many cases, remain in the hospital bed until their eventual death.

For many of these patients, members of the medical staff who are responsible for the treatment of these unfortunate victims of the COVID-19 virus are essentially adopted family members. It matters how the perishing patient will live out their remaining time on earth. An individual who is severely stricken with COVID-19 should be treated with the utmost dignity and respect.

Because there are so many either perishing or on the brink of death due to this pandemic, I can also understand the perspective of some working on the front lines in the COVID-19 battle. It is suggested and highly recommended that each member of a medical staff conduct themselves in a professional manner. They cannot become emotionally attached to anyone entering treatment.

Those who are caring for the infected patient must walk a fine line between professionalism, love, and empathy. It is human nature to become saddened when anyone loses one's life. The frontline worker in the midst of a chaotic environment with patient after patient, entering the battle-tested grounds of a hospital, is overwhelmed by the continuous carousel of individuals who have been severely stricken with the virus.

No amount of money can substitute for the reward that a medical staff experiences when an individual has recovered and is strong enough to become one of the few individuals who have overcome this viral epidemic. If there is one small victory for those who put their lives in danger each day while caring for the COVID-19 patient, it is when the patient cheats a potential death and defies the odds. An individual who was hospitalized due to the viral pandemic will hopefully regain one's health again by maintaining the right amount of hope and optimism.

Do you know who is most looking forward and anticipating the day that COVID-19 will not have any prolonged effect in our world and society? I believe that it is the doctors, nurses, and medical staff members who will rejoice when they are no longer in the midst of peril and stress. Some who have been caring for the infected COVID-19 patient have not experienced any quality downtime. Those who care for individuals who have contacted the virus are also hopeful for a long-lasting solution to the COVID-19 health battle.

Enduring the COVID-19 virus for the past several months has many wondering if there is an ending in sight. It is both painful and heartbreaking to hear the news of how COVID-19 has destroyed families. I can recall watching a television program and learning about a five-year-old boy who lost his parents to this deadly virus.

Now he has to be raised by a family member. This is one of the many examples of this pandemic changing a family's dynamic. COVID-19 is like a devastating storm that terrorizes a town.

The aftermath of the storm, in many cases, results in life-altering consequences. A weather disturbance might be long gone, but the individuals who are affected by it are forced to adjust and restart their lives. COVID-19 is a disease that will also wreck the lives of many of the individuals who have contracted it as well as the life of an infected individual.

Those who have experienced the utter chaos and destruction of COVID-19 will welcome the day when the disease is no longer a threat to the world and humanity. Although this virus is a serious disease epidemic, there is hope that it will lose its strong influence over the lives of many. I am eager and hopeful to see how this viral pandemic will factor in the lives of millions in the coming years.

Is this an epidemic that is a temporary cause for concern, or is it a passing health crisis which will soon become a thing of the past? Regardless of the duration of this illness, it has resulted in a priority change for millions of people. In some instances, the COVID-19 virus has helped some appreciate life. Many have learned through the onset of this deadly pandemic that life is fragile.

What will happen to our world and society if the battle with the COVID-19 virus is won? I believe that some might savor another chance to live a full life, while others could potentially return to the error of their ways. Whatever the case may be, every individual living in these unprecedented times will welcome the day that COVID-19 is no longer destroying every facet of life.

Once this viral pestilence is controlled, I hope that many will realize how fortunate and blessed they are. The COVID-19 virus could have potentially wiped out the majority of the United States. Some government officials have been accepting of what would be needed to get this deadly virus under control.

As valued members of society, each life is important and vital. Because of this pandemic, no one should take one's life or any other life as not being special. COVID-19 has personally taught me that life is always flowing in cycles and waves.

Our world and nation has experienced a wave of death and utter destruction. One cannot predict how potent and deadly the next potential threat of life could affect the individuals who have survived being stricken with COVID-19. While we cannot fully prepare for what is to come in our world, we do have a chance to leave this devastating disease behind.

Who could have predicted that we as a nation would be battling a severe and potential deadly infectious disease? I am aware that there have been movies made in the past chronicling a potential outbreak.

When COVID-19 initially surfaced, some thought that it was only an isolated incident which only affected a particular segment of society. No one could have imagined how this small virus particle would affect the world in the way that it has.

In our nation, we are not used to many perishing from any type of health crisis at an alarming and increasing rate. The United States has usually been an example of a country that could boast about not having illnesses and diseases which could affect millions of its citizens. If you were to tell me that America, one of the leading countries in the world in regard to medical technology, would be the leading nation in the amount of deaths from a viral pandemic, I would have questioned your sanity.

Although there are other nations worldwide that are also having difficulties with this pandemic, the United States, thus far, is powerless in regard to the spread of the disease. There is hope that COVID-19 will soon become an illness which will no longer have precedence. Until these current vaccines become widespread, it is imperative that all who contract the virus do not lose faith that a vaccine will not only become available to all but also significantly effective.

At this present moment, it does seem promising that we as a nation will be able to move past the destruction of the COVID-19 virus. The advantage that the United States has in its favor is the fact there are leading experts and drug companies in this nation that are more than capable of reducing the threat of this virus with a vaccine that is potent. I cannot comment on other medical experts in various nations, but I am confident that the scientists and the infectious disease experts in America can hugely affect the negative numbers in the COVID-19 battle.

I am amazed about how rapidly there have been vaccines created in this viral pandemic battle. As I stated previously, many will have the option of choosing more than one vaccine in the prevention of contracting COVID-19. This news is both positive as well as a game changer in regard to combating this viral epidemic.

One day, the COVID-19 viral pandemic could lose its reign of terror on millions of people worldwide. Living in the era of this global pandemic will have one longing for those days of living without masks and physical distancing. As we all await the availability of vaccines distributed throughout this world and nation, there is hope that an individual can still enjoy life without experiencing anxiety over this widespread infectious disease.

Optimism and patience will prevail when the COVID-19 virus is no longer a significant factor in our society. If one could continue to exhibit optimism in the midst of negative circumstances, then a reward will come into fruition. In regard to the COVID-19 viral pandemic, do not cease anticipating the day in which the epidemic will no longer cause destruction and fear.

CHAPTER 8

Responding to COVID-19

Many people are not who they used to be before the onset of this pandemic. What I mean is that some have allowed this viral outbreak to negatively affect their personality. An individual who was once an easygoing optimist is now an anxious and stress-filled pessimist.

Some individuals cannot consistently have an optimistic outlook on life when the world around them is in shambles. As the pandemic is increasingly taking the lives of millions worldwide, many living through these difficult times are filled with hopelessness. This has had a domino effect on others.

Have you interacted with other individuals during these unpleasant times? The majority of individuals who happen to be out and about are unfriendly. It is disheartening to experience those with negative personalities. I believe that individuals who respond to trials and difficulties in a negative way do not have enough faith that there can be a better outcome.

The COVID-19 virus is responsible for having a plethora of people unloading their frustrations on other unsuspecting individuals. I do not understand how someone could unleash pain and harm toward others when we all are experiencing this negative disease together. One would think that an individual who has a pessimistic attitude and personality would be grateful to be alive.

How are you responding to the COVID-19 virus? I hope you understand that this virus is not anyone's fault. If one can have the mindset that the COVID-19 virus originally spread without any full warning to many in this nation and all around the world, then one could respond more positively. Trials and difficulties in life are impossible to avoid.

What is different about this virus as opposed to other pestilences that have plagued society is how it has affected every single individual in it in some type of way. There were other health crises which did not result in approximately a full year of trials and misfortune for a country such as the United States. This is why the personalities of many are not as positively infectious.

As a nation, we are not accustomed to experiencing prolonged infectious disease epidemics and pandemics. Due to this continuous battle, some have allowed their personality to become influenced by the ongoing trial of COVID-19. When we are in the midst of a difficult time in our life, we become unaware how much our personalities are affected.

I am not oblivious to the fact that the COVID-19 virus is not a disease which will have the individual who contracts it jump for joy. It is an illness that will typically have one in a somber type of mood. In my opinion, an individual's mindset and personality is both vital and crucial in combating and overcoming COVID-19.

Your personality should not be altered because of the COVID-19 virus. If you have a bubbly personality, then continue to be that person. Do not allow this virus to change the individual that you are personality wise.

Sadness and anxiety fill the air now that we are in the constant battle over life and death. I must say that I can empathize with how and why one would have those feelings. Dealing with the COVID-19 virus for all these months can make the happiest person in the world become depressed.

As an individual who has battled and become victorious over emotional issues in the past, I am thankful that I have not allowed this pandemic to influence my feelings and emotions. The way that I have personally responded to the COVID-19 virus crisis is by viewing it as another necessary trial which must be dealt with in life.

Just because I have been able to keep my emotions in check does not mean that I am not bothered or saddened by the plethora of lives that were taken due to this terrible outbreak. Though I have never experienced a pestilence like COVID-19 in my lifetime, I must say that my response to it was not shocking. For several years, I have seen chaos, turmoil, and utter destruction affect the fabric of our world and society.

With this nation steadily on a moral decline for several decades by disregarding the significance and importance of the Creator, I knew that something drastic would affect this country in a negative way. Now I did not foresee a viral pandemic on the horizon, but I knew that some type of trial or mishap would affect the entire country deeply.

It is okay to have grieve in one's life, particularly in this unforeseen circumstance. Every individual has varying ways of responding to grief from a crisis. Some choose to internalize their feelings of grief, while others outwardly bash others.

No matter how you have responded to this global pandemic, it does not change the fact that it is both a national and global crisis. An individual living during this unprecedented era is never alone in one's grief, especially in this unusual situation. There are millions around the world who feel deep hopelessness and sadness because this virus has robbed friends and loved ones of time and being alive.

There should not be any surprise when the amount of individuals experiencing depression and anxiety has not only increased in this country but also worldwide. One does not know how they will respond to negative and catastrophic events when they occur suddenly and unexpectedly. If you have not experienced some feelings of concern or sadness due to this pandemic, then you are not a living, breathing, human being.

On the other hand, an individual should also respond to this virus with bravery and courage. I am cognizant of the fact that this type of response is not always typical while in the midst of a life-threatening epidemic. One must dig deep from within to have a courageous response to COVID-19.

This difficult and life-altering pandemic has caused many to respond in fear and sadness. As a result of those feelings, a plethora of individuals living during these difficult and uncertain times cannot experience peace. In regard to one's response to the COVID-19 virus, it is understandable when an individual experiences all the emotions of grief.

Despite all the grim news about the global pandemic, one must maintain an optimistic and hopeful attitude. Though there is promising potential that the virus may not cause as much harm in the future due to the development of vaccines to combat it, one should try to remain composed if one is ever stricken with the illness. It will not do anyone any good to automatically declare defeat if one happens to contract the disease.

As a nation, we have responded in an unfavorable way to COVID-19. Some considered the virus a hoax when it initially spread. Due to this mindset, the COVID-19 virus has become a thorn in the side in this country ever since. It has been proven that a lukewarm response to how serious this pandemic is has been one of the main reasons why COVID-19 skyrocketed vastly.

Also, some of the leaders in our country turned the other cheek when the virus commenced to become a larger issue. Because many influential government officials initially did not see any cause for concern, the United States became divided in regard to responding to the viral outbreak. I believe that we as a nation have paid a huge price by our attitudes and response to the epidemic collectively.

I am disappointed by the apathetic mindsets of some. If this country has any chance of taming this virus, each citizen must not respond to it with complacency. With the news of vaccines, some have responded in extreme hope, while others have responded in extreme skepticism.

Recently I have seen some celebrities carrying on as if there was not any deadly pandemic in the world. These men and women of fame are sending out mixed messages. When an individual is a famous celebrity, they must become aware of how a plethora of individuals will be influenced by what they do or say.

Seeing individuals of influence disregard how serious this infectious disease is by carousing in nightclubs without face coverings or physical distancing relays the message to wide-eyed fans that the COVID-19 virus does not pose any type of potential threat. If these influential celebrities could alter their responses to COVID-19, I believe that the virus will eventually become controlled. This does not mean that the virus itself will suddenly disappear, but with millions of people responding to the virus by cooperating with doctors and experts, we can defy the odds in regard to this pandemic despite the grim news.

It is imperative that everyone in this nation and worldwide are on the same page when it comes to their response to COVID-19. Yes, there are vaccines that are readily available to the masses. Although these vaccines have the potential of many breathing a sigh of relief, it still does not mean that everyone should not respond to the virus without caution.

Let's face it: the United States is behind other nations with inferior medical technology due to the lackadaisical response to a highly contagious disease. We have to have more than just a hopeful and optimistic response to the potential of a decline in COVID-19 cases. One must still adhere to guidelines and instructions on this viral disease.

Frontline healthcare workers are to be commended for their tireless efforts and care for those who are in the battle of their lives due to COVID-19. Many of the men and women in these positions have responded to this virus wholeheartedly without any questions asked. Some have been successful in nursing the COVID-19 patients to health, while others have not been as fortunate. How many of us could work a sixteen-hour shift approximately seven days a week, full-time for over a year?

Also, to make matters worse, the worker's medical team as well as the patients who are depending on the worker expect these individuals to have a positive attitude and response each day in a dire situation. Caring and responding to victims of this virus requires a plethora of mental stability. It is fair for me to state that the frontline health worker is often overlooked and overworked.

Some of the responders to the COVID-19 virus are expected to report to work each day while suppressing their feelings and emotions. These individuals might also experience fear and depression due to the continuous trauma of losing many individuals from this viral nightmare. One must never disregard how difficult and challenging it is to respond to individuals who are infected with the virus.

A healthcare worker who is responding to COVID-19 must not only serve and protect those battling the disease, but they also must protect themselves from also contracting and succumbing to the pestilence. I can only imagine the constant physical and mental toll, in which many of the frontline essential healthcare workers experience, when it comes to caring for the stricken patient. This could be detrimental to the health of the worker, but I am certain that they feel obligated to continue to press on.

An individual serving on the front lines in the COVID-19 battle views it as an opportunity to help others to become comfortable in spite of the hurt and pain that this virus has caused. Responders in the viral battle must also become an amateur therapist or psychiatrist in addition to caring for those severely affected by the COVID-19 virus. A patient with a serious case of COVID-19 must feel as though the responder has their best interest.

Hopefully, in the near future, there will be a minimal amount of individuals who will not have the crucial task of caring and responding to those with COVID-19 issues. As of now, it remains to be seen whether or not responding to individuals who are stricken with the virus will become less of a concern. The only thing that a frontline healthcare responder can do is to somehow find the strength and courage to fulfill their duties to the best of one's God-given ability.

Patients hospitalized due to COVID-19 and frontline health care workers are basically intertwined with one another. It is imperative that the workers and responders of the COVID-19 virus continue to serve and care with dignity. Besides a loving family, a loving responder is always needed.

What is the best way of responding to any crisis? I believe that one must respond in faith. The COVID-19 virus has tested an individual's spiritual discipline. It is difficult to maintain one's focus on the Creator when there is so much turmoil and death.

Just because COVID-19 is causing great destruction, one must have the faith that this difficult chapter in our world's history will one day pass. Currently it does not look promising that this virus might subside and diminish. The death toll from COVID-19 is almost as much as the total amount of residents residing in the city of New Orleans.

There are some who are stricken with the disease who do not realize that they have contracted this mysterious virus. These particular individuals might, by chance, happen to discover the revelation that they are infected. Our local and national news has painted a grim picture in regard to an individual who contracts COVID-19.

Because of the national perception of the COVID-19 virus, many do not have enough faith that if they happen to hypothetically contract the disease, that there chance of survival is not minuscule. Some do not realize that although currently the efficacy of these vaccines is to be determined, there are still some who have victoriously recovered from the virus. Individuals who have survived this debilitating disease have had the faith that they will be healed.

If one happens to become infected with COVID-19, that individual should automatically respond in faith. Though the odds of contracting the virus is great, one must have the mindset that one will eventually get better. In my own life, I have battled illnesses in which most thought that I could never have overcome.

As a child, I battled a severe bout with asthma. During physical education class each week, I would always find myself in the nurse's office after a grueling workout. My asthma attacks were the result of my all-out effort.

One day, I commenced to look forward to my visit with the nurse after an intense workout. What occurred next is an unforeseen miracle. It was my eighth grade year in middle school, and I was able to do all the physical activities in my physical education class without any issue with asthma.

This occurred over thirty-plus years ago, and I have not had an asthma attack since I was a youth. My condition has improved immensely due to two reasons. One reason why I was able to overcome asthma is because my bout with the illness was a childhood case of it. Fortunately, I was able to grow out of it.

Another reason why I defied the odds in overcoming my childhood experience is because of my response to the illness. Though experiencing childhood asthma was a terrifying experience at times, I chose to respond to the condition with faith. I developed the faith that one day I would overcome the ailment and become physically fit and not have to experience any more attacks. In regard to the COVID-19 virus, one must respond to the illness in faith that they too can survive it.

Approaching the COVID-19 virus in an apathetic way demonstrates immaturity. There are some who refuse to accept the fact that COVID-19 is a dangerous-and-threatening condition to human life. Still some do not take heed to what is happening in their communities as well as in society.

I have personally seen individuals who do not take the proper precautions when it comes to staying healthy. Instead of wearing some type of protective gear, some chose to carry on as if there was not any cause for concern. These particular individuals are arrogant and defiant.

Choosing to respond to wearing a mask with disdain, or responding in disgust when experts and officials suggest to the public to not have a plethora of individuals in one's home is very childlike in my opinion. Only children have a negative response over things that they care not to do. Seeing mature and perfectly able adults who are able to comprehend instructions defy what is required by sage health experts on the issue of the COVID-19 virus, I must say, is disappointing.

Many will risk their lives by not wearing a mask or physically distancing because it is viewed as inconvenient. Because of a minor inconvenience, some are willing to pay a potentially deadly price in order to experience temporary comfort. I believe that one is demonstrating growth and maturity when one follows as well as makes the effort to do what is required to carry out the protocol.

Wearing a mask or face covering and physical distancing is difficult. Face coverings can be very uncomfortable. Many complain that their breathing is restricted.

In some instances, I can fathom why wearing protective gear is bothersome to wear. On the contrary, a little discomfort and sacrifice is better than potentially contracting the virus. I am confident that many of the individuals who have negatively responded to all the mandatory safety precautions in regard to the COVID-19 virus would tell others, after losing the battle with the disease, that wearing those uncomfortable masks and face coverings is definitely worth it.

There are a plethora of things in life that I would rather not do, but I know that I have to do those things because I would like to be a responsible adult. It is all part of growth and maturity in life when one has to sacrifice a moment of want or desire over doing what might prove to become beneficial. In regard to the COVID-19 virus, one might not desire to follow all the guidelines and requirements in the protection from the epidemic, but one will do it anyway if it means that one will have a greater chance of not becoming infected.

Mature men and women do what is needed in order to maintain a high level in regard to one's quality of life. Responding favorably to the requirements suggested by experts and government officials can help each individual who is willing to carry out that sacrifice. A positive response to the COVID-19 protocols can become difficult to do, but it could eventually determine whether one lives or dies during this viral pandemic.

One does not realize how much courage and strength one has until one is thrust into a chaotic situation. The COVID-19 virus is the catalyst for some to transition from an individual with limited courage to someone who relishes a challenge. It is imperative that an individual learns how to respond to trials and difficulties in life with a positive mindset.

Some have opted to allow this virus to consume them. Now I am not saying that one should not become concerned about the potential of contracting the disease because it can be deadly. Personally, I believe that an individual should do all that one can to not become stricken with the virus, but beyond taking all of the necessary precautions, there is little else in which one can do.

The only real response that one must have if one is ever afflicted with COVID-19 is to remember the Almighty. If you believe in your heart that He can heal you from a potential life-threatening disease, then you have responded the way that the Father would like you to respond. I am aware that only the Creator and Messiah has the power to determine whether or not one will be able to overcome and heal from the virus.

An individual must believe in one's heart that one always has at least somewhat of a chance to become victorious in just about any negative situation. If one has that mindset, he or she will respond with a hopeful attitude. Many do not realize how one's response to a negative situation or circumstance could become the difference between survival and one's demise.

Despite what seems to be occurring in this nation, there is always the possibility that an illness such as COVID-19 can become less of a threat to the world and society. One must not focus on what is happening currently, but one should have one's mindset on a world which will one day become void of illnesses that results in chaos and anxiety. An individual who becomes stricken with the COVID-19 virus must be accepting of whatever fate that life has in store for them.

Sure, it is difficult to accept that our life could become cut short due to this pandemic. No one can negotiate one's time on earth. The best thing that anyone can do is, trust the fact that our loving Creator always knows what is best for us.

When someone is aware of one's own limited mortality, then that individual will have a more peaceful and calmer response to having a negative situation occurring in one's life. I am not saying that one should give up the battle for one's strength and health. My suggestion to those striving to overcome the COVID-19 virus is to never limit your potential strength in dealing with the severity of the sickness.

Each individual should respond with courage while battling this illness. One must strive not to respond to the adversity and hardship of this virus with self-pity while not yielding to it. Hope and optimism should be the mindset if one is fortunate enough to survive the disease, or even if the battle is unfortunately lost in the end.

Striving to obtain knowledge of an illness or disease is beneficial. When an individual is able to acquire as much information as possible in regard to an illness, then that can give the individual crucial ammunition to combat it. Instead of responding to being infected with the COVID-19 virus with worry and anxiety, one can arm oneself with a plethora of knowledge.

This virus is a disease that is new and unfamiliar to many in our society. We are discovering facts about the COVID-19 virus with each passing day. It is imperative that all who are living in this era of the COVID-19 virus acquire knowledge about it instead of being passive.

Sometimes many of us react negatively to a situation or circumstance when we do not understand what is happening. I believe that a plethora of individuals in this country and elsewhere have allowed themselves to respond negatively to this viral outbreak due to unfamiliarity. It is human nature to exhibit an unfavorable reaction to situations and circumstances which are beyond our grasp.

Those who have played or been involved in sports are aware that there is always a scouting report on the opponent. In the scouting report, there are revelations about what the opponent likes to do within a game. Basically, a viable scouting report will list and reveal those tendencies, which a team might not be aware that it does.

A good team that pays attention to the scouting report are better equipped to win the game after learning the opponent's favorite tendencies and plays. The team has acquired the needed knowledge to master their opponent. When a team does not have a reliable scouting report, typically it results in the team losing and being dominated by the opposing team.

As a society, we have to adopt that same mentality in regard to the COVID-19 virus. I am cognizant of the fact that the stakes are higher than a game that is for entertainment purposes. Lives around this nation and world are in jeopardy. Regardless of the significance of the current situation which we are now currently experiencing and facing, this viral outbreak is an uphill battle.

The experts have given us the scouting report on COVID-19. We know that it can be contracted on surfaces and through human interaction. Also, the individuals with knowledge on infectious diseases have revealed the various ways in which the virus could be spread because they did their due diligence on the disease by studying the tendencies of this particular pestilence.

Scouting the COVID-19 virus has proved to be a key factor in minimizing it in the past. There were a few months that it seemed as though the battle with this invisible threat was subsiding in this nation, as well as worldwide. Many of the citizens in this country know what to do in regard to this virus, but refuse to study the scouting report on the disease given by experts. It is up to us as a nation and society to recognize the tendencies of this viral outbreak because all the scouting information on this virus that is available to all proves that there is not any excuse when it comes to victory and mastery over this viral threat.

Fear is the prevailing emotion that many are demonstrating during these times of the pandemic. I do not blame those who have become anxious due to this virus. If one is not careful, this infectious disease has the potential to claim one's life mentally.

Though it is understandable for one to have some semblance of fear, this negative emotion must not have prolonged dominance. If fear continues to dominate an individual, eventually it will result in anxiety and, perhaps, a mental breakdown. Because many are in constant fear of contracting the COVID-19 virus, a majority of individuals living in our world and society are mentally affected.

We all must become mentally in tune with our feelings and emotions. I know that it is difficult to maintain one's mental health when there are so many people perishing from this viral epidemic. The news media has made matters worse by reporting on the astronomical toll.

How can someone ease the fear of those living in this current era? I believe that a relationship with a reliable man or woman of God will definitely help one's feelings of fear. Some might suggest online therapy to help those fearful emotions subside. In both instances, I recommend that one express their feelings of fear and anxiety to someone who will be that listening ear.

No one should live with a fearful mindset. Responding to life's difficulties in fear will compound the issue. One has to have a clear conscience when encountering challenging matters. Although one might have a clear mind, it does not change the fact that there is a deadly pandemic threatening humanity.

When an individual has followed the guidelines in the prevention of becoming infected with COVID-19, that individual will have no need to respond to the virus in a worrisome fashion. One must strive to avoid being fearful in regard to this viral outbreak. Remember what I stated in a previous chapter about the law of attraction.

We tend to inadvertently attract things within our own realm. For example, if you have a fear of dogs, and a dog just so happens to come around you, that fear could be sensed by the animal. I hope that the only result from that sense of fear from that dog is a bark.

In some cases, an individual's fear could turn into a clear reality when one's law of attraction is involved. Some might say that their worst fears have now come into fruition. The COVID-19 virus could be that law of attraction for the individual who is in constant fear and worry.

It is as though one's fear could serve as the catalyst for an individual contracting COVID-19. I do not recommend that individuals living in the viral pandemic era avoid the fact that a viral threat is in existence. One would be foolish to have an attitude of denial, which could ultimately prove costly in regard to one's life. Individuals with a fearful mindset must not fear an illness when one is doing what the experts have asked of them.

Ultimately, we have control about whether or not a response of courage or fear will have precedence over our emotions in regard to COVID-19. Those who have a realistic response to COVID-19 are more able to understand how most pestilences occur in our world. Responding to the COVID-19 virus realistically could help an individual encounter these chaotic circumstances.

Many who are responding to this viral outbreak in an apathetic way do not understand how harmful this mindset is. Because of this mindset, this virus spread like wildfire among all the fifty states in America. Some are regretful in their approach and response to this pandemic, while others are oblivious to how potentially deadly and life-altering that contracting this virus can become.

There is always hope that one's response to the virus could be vastly different in due time. Hopefully, one's response to how detrimental the disease is does not change when the individual is on his or her deathbed. This is when one's response to how harmful becoming infected with the virus is a little too late.

One benefit of fear is that it will influence some to go above and beyond to protect oneself. COVID-19 has influenced some to be more cautious and careful in regard to their own hygienic habits and cleanliness. Instead of grumbling about the amount of soap and hand sanitizer that one uses, one should respond with gratitude in regard to how one is able to use products to help alleviate the potential of becoming afflicted with the disease.

As a nation and society, we have been through an enormous amount of challenges and difficulties due to this invisible threat. One of the main reasons why our country has experienced great heartache and pain is because of our own ignorant responses to what experts and government officials tried to warn each citizen. Those who have chosen to respond ignorantly to helpful advice may now realize how wrong it was for them to negatively react to what is now one of three current-leading causes of death in our depleted nation.

Optimistically, we all can learn from the lessons in our response to the COVID-19 virus. It is imperative that each individual residing in these times of pestilences and diseases has a better response to warnings. I believe that our nation would not be in the state and predicament that it is in if more individuals would have been more receptive to the warnings of the infectious disease experts.

The bottom line is that we have a pandemic that came right out of the blue. Due to the suddenness of this worldwide phenomenon, no one could have understood the need to rely upon our responses, as well as individuals who are well-qualified to comment on what has to be done to overcome this long, dragged-out battle with COVID-19. Now that there are vaccines, which are slowly becoming available to the masses for distribution, it is now time to have a positive and favorable response in following the guidelines while carrying out the preventive precautions of this invisible enemy.

CHAPTER 9

Be Inspired

Drawing inspiration from others is essential in overcoming this devastating outbreak. Although there is a plethora of negative news in the headlines, individuals can also become inspired by those who have been in the midst of this pandemic. Doctors and individuals who have overcome being infected with the virus are prime examples of inspiration of those who have been dealing nonstop with this epidemic.

In the genesis of this epidemic, the elderly population was severely affected by the COVID-19 virus. A great amount of individuals living in assisted living were perishing as a result of contracting the virus. During the initial outbreak of the pandemic, it seemed as though an individual over sixty-five had little to no chance of surviving becoming infected with COVID-19.

As the pandemic has surged in other age groups, some of the individuals in the elderly population have been able to defy the odds and recover. I have seen individuals as old as one hundred years of age survive this deadly disease. When someone is able to survive all that encompasses being stricken with COVID-19, it is amazing how any individual at any age could battle the illness and win.

It is more remarkable and inspiring when an elderly individual over the age of ninety can come out on the positive side of a potentially life-threatening virus. Those who are in the battle with COVID-19 can be inspired by the tenacity of individuals who many would assume could not overcome the symptoms and side effects of the illness. Inspiration in defeating this viral threat is vital for each individual afflicted who might be having a difficult time in one's experience with the pestilence.

When it comes to being inspired, one can also become inspired by oneself. Some individuals have been through an enormous amount of trials and difficulties in this life. Individuals who were able to survive a negative ordeal can find it within themselves to become inspired and motivated.

Recently there was an elderly couple that became stricken with the COVID-19 virus. They both resided in the same nursing home. Because the facility in which they resided in became overwhelmed with numerous cases of COVID-19, this particular couple had to become separated.

The couple with whom I am referring to have never experienced a day apart since they were married many years ago. After several months of separation, both recovered from the virus and became reunited together again. I believe that it requires a great deal of strength and courage to survive a life-threatening disease while being separated from an individual whom you love and do not have any information about their whereabouts.

These men and women, with whom I have just discussed, are inspirations of hope and courage. It takes a great amount of positive thoughts to fight a disease battle while being isolated from the love of your life at the same time. If a seasoned couple can overcome COVID-19, then we all have a chance of overcoming the illness and also becoming inspired.

Feeding the mind with news of hope will definitely result in an individual having thoughts of inspiration. With the continuous negative coverage on the COVID-19 virus, being inspired should become a top priority. Sometimes the past can help one with inspirational thoughts.

As a nation, we must reflect back to our past for hope and inspiration from the negative circumstances in which we are currently encountering. The United States has been through many devastating events in its history. Each time a difficult or negative occurrence was in danger of destroying our country, we have been able to overcome the mishap.

Right now, our nation, as well as the world, is in need of a psychological boost. All the chaos, destruction, and death from this virus are cause for inspirational acts by those who are able to do it. It is our tendency as human beings to desire some type of emotional trigger that will help us in times of extreme difficulty.

No one can gain inspiration from tuning in to the increasing death toll and the number of individuals becoming infected with the COVID-19 virus daily. Hopefully one can view stories of uplifting news in order to experience hopeful and optimistic emotions. The men and women who have been able to move on in life after losing their jobs, homes, and sometimes health are the real uplifting stories of exalting influence.

Personally, I am inspired by the doctors, as well as nurses, who have given time and their talents to individuals in need of inspiration. Imagine not having any time for recreational activities because you are committed in your quest to save as many lives as you can. Many who are in the battle with COVID-19 from a health worker's perspective are expected to inspire their perishing patients to live while inwardly losing their own battle with motivating themselves to care for a seemingly never-ending trial.

It is imperative that we strive to also inspire and motivate those who are on the front lines of the COVID-19 battle. How can we inspire individuals in the midst of an uncontrollable pandemic? I believe that the best way that these brave men and women can become inspired is by demonstrating that you care for them and others. The first thing I think a front line healthcare worker would tell you is to follow all the guidelines and requirements recommended by experts so they will not have to unfortunately see you in the ICU (Intensive Care Unit).

Workers battling the COVID-19 virus in hospitals in the U.S. and worldwide would be inspired themselves when, collectively, each individual is not stubborn and defiant in regard to wearing protective gear and following precautions. This would mean that their jobs could potentially become less harmful and stressful. It really matters how inspired and motivated individuals in the healthcare field are.

If these workers are not inspired in some way to do their jobs, then they will not be able to properly care for those battling COVID-19. Every individual must be inspired to do one's best. Those on the front lines in the COVID-19 battle are not exempt from also experiencing inspiration.

Envisioning stability during these unprecedented times can become challenging. As a mere human, I cannot predict or profess to know if our world and society will be able to return to the way it was pre-pandemic. The only thing that we can do while living in the COVID-19 era is live one's life the best and honest way that one knows how.

We all are inspirations to ourselves when there is another day to live. The COVID-19 virus is an illness that is least likely to result in individuals becoming inspired, but it has also been inspiring for many when they combat and overcome it. There is so much grim and negative news in our world today that has nothing to do with the virus itself.

It is imperative that each individual living in the COVID-19 era seek inspiration from someone or something. In my opinion, an individual who is inspired is more productive. Some are not motivated to do anything because of orders from local government officials to either remain at home or limit their exposure to the outside world.

An individual who is not inspired is literally someone who has the potential to remain in a stagnate position. This virus has caused many to give up on their goals and dreams. I can empathize with the individual who is unable to achieve their aspirations.

COVID-19 has put the majority of individuals' dreams on hold. Due to this unfavorable circumstance, some are disheartened. It is difficult to obtain inspiration when the world and environment around you is shut down.

One must never allow oneself to become uninspired. As a result of COVID-19, there are residual effects of individuals losing their way in life. Some have resorted to petty crime in order to fill the void of lack and helplessness.

Because of many living uninspired lives, our world and society has been negatively affected by this unfavorable mindset. Hope and inspiration is now replaced by pessimism. When a society as a whole is filled with negative attitudes, the individuals living in it will suffer the consequences.

Our world and nation needs inspiration and optimism, though adversity is prevalent. Being inspired in these times can be accomplished. Inspiration commences and ends within an individual.

If each individual could become inspired by hope of the virus ceasing, then there is a chance that optimism will return. I believe that one should inspire oneself to have visions of stability. Society as we know it may or may not become consistently stable, but you can achieve it internally.

Focusing on what inspires us will positively affect the morale of our society. Hopefully there will be a day in our world and society when this will occur. With the difficulties in which many have encountered due to this viral outbreak, it will be a welcomed experience to have individuals living inspired lives in spite of the uninspiring behavior of society as a whole.

Faith is definitely something that one can acquire inspiration from. Our heavenly Father can turn any situation that might seem bleak into a victorious one. Only God can ultimately heal an individual who might have a slight chance of survival from the COVID-19 virus.

One's belief in the Creator and His Son, Jesus Christ, is one's reliable source of inspiration. Now I do believe that doctors and nurses can help an individual regain health and healing, but only the Father, Himself, has the power and authority to grant an individual strength, courage, and hope to combat a disease that is so harmful and threatening to the lives of millions. If those who are battling the disease are inspired by the healing of our Creator, then the virus will not alter one's faith—that one can battle and overcome it.

In my lifetime, I have seen situations that seemed as though it would result in an unfavorable circumstance and, suddenly, become favorable as a result of faith and inspiration. Think about it. It is an act of God to have individuals heal who are deemed as unlikely to survive an infectious disease. Only the Creator who can inspire and motivate those who were not given any chance of overcoming COVID-19 hope to be able to enjoy life again.

Those who are spiritually driven understand that healing is supernatural. Some might suggest that their doctors and members of the medical staff are responsible for total healing from the virus. Sure, those working on the front lines of this pandemic should be given some credit for helping nurse individuals stricken with the COVID-19 virus back to health.

The question that I pose to anyone who thinks that a doctor or nurse is solely and ultimately responsible for all of one's healing from the COVID-19 virus is, "Who gave the doctors and the nurses taking care of the infected individual the wisdom to know how to help an embattled patient overcome a newly and little-known mysterious virus?" When the COVID-19 virus became widespread, there were members of medical staffs in this country and around the world that did not know how to properly treat those infected with the illness. In many cases, it was a trial and error treatment of the virus for doctors and nurses.

This proves my point that the Creator is the one who provides the knowledge to those searching for answers to the relatively unknown. As this viral disease spread throughout the world, many were oblivious to the fact that a deadly virus could be the source for inspiration. COVID-19 is an example of how our heavenly Father can inspire some individuals to have more empathy toward others who might be different from another individual in some way.

There are some who have survived COVID-19 who, in many cases, defied death. Some have been in the care of nurses and doctors for a substantial amount of time. When some of the survivors of COVID-19 entered the ICU, I am certain that they themselves thought that there was not any way out of this dire situation.

Previously, I discussed how an individual could be inspired by unlikely individuals who have overcome COVID-19. In the unpredictable climate in which we are living in, every individual needs to experience inspiration. It is inspiring to see how some have come together to care for the most vulnerable population, which is the homeless.

When the virus initially surfaced, I have seen some of my local government officials express concern for those who are less fortunate and down on their luck. The mayor, along with other city officials, braved the elements and handed individuals who are not in the position to take care of themselves gloves and masks to protect them from the virus. There are some who are in positions of influence and power who do not consider that element of the population, which is typically forgotten.

I reside in the Houston area, and although this city is not the city I was born in, I must say that many of the people who reside in this city are inspiring to me. Not only are the current mayor and city health experts, men and women of exceptional character from my perspective—all of them have demonstrated leadership and courage in the midst of a negative occurrence. Day after day, I have seen how proactive these individuals have become in the COVID-19 battle.

Now I do not personally know these local government officials, but I have become inspired by their concern as well as the assertive mentality of these individuals. I can recall a period in the COVID-19 battle when the fourth largest city in America, Houston, Texas, was among the lowest in the country in regard to citizens stricken with the COVID-19 virus. During that time, this was quite an accomplishment.

The rate of individuals recovering from the infectious disease increased in my local area when it was mandatory and suggested that the majority of the population remain at home. There were many in the medical field that had to learn, as they progressed along, how to care for the infected individual with COVID-19; and frankly, I find that remarkable. I believe that many individuals who have accepted the fact that an invisible viral pandemic was severe enough to close down industries of commerce should be commended. Human lives are more important than a thriving economy.

It was an unpopular decision to cease operations of businesses in the fourth largest city in the entire nation. Although the difficult decision to shut down restaurants and many essential businesses has greatly affected the local and national economy, I believe, in hindsight, that it was a necessary thing to do at that time. In order for the viral outbreak to subside, there had to be a drastic measure which had to be taken.

I must admit that I am not the most politically driven individual, but I am the most inspired one. Not only did my local area take the needed precautions to preserve the lives of its citizens, but other cities and states across the country also chose life over profit. Some have grumbled and complained because they were not able to make a living.

This reaction is understandable because if one cannot make a living, then that individual and their family cannot survive. It takes a plethora of courage to go against the grain. I am inspired by the fact that some individuals in positions of power chose life over popularity.

Honestly, due to the utter destruction as a result of this pandemic, many have had little to become inspired by. An individual doing the most basic and essential activities is constantly reminded that we are in the midst of a global and viral disease epidemic. For example, when we go to the local supermarket to shop for groceries, there are signs in some stores which emphasize the point that we must physically distance ourselves from one another.

How can one experience joy when the environment around us is a constant reminder of what we are currently experiencing as a world and society? I believe that joy and inspiration are choices that we internally make. On the contrary, an individual can also decide whether or not to remain in a negative state of mind. Thus far, I have discussed how one can become inspired by either internal or external factors.

The world in which we live is increasingly becoming more negative and uninspiring. As valued members of the world and society, it is imperative that we seek inspiration from previous experiences in life. With the world becoming more perilous each day, with or without a viral pandemic, it is understandable why many are not receiving inspiration within their minds and hearts.

Just like it is vital for one to have at least three square meals within a day, it is also imperative that one experiences some form of daily inspiration. Personally, I am inspired by joy. Being inspired by joy in one's life can influence one to have a positive attitude regardless of the situation or circumstances.

One has to look no further than the Word of God to become inspired. His Word is definitely responsible for an individual maintaining a consistent level of joy and inspiration in spite of the pessimistic worldly view on events and phenomenon, such as the COVID-19 virus. Whenever anyone needs a pick-me-up, the Bible is just the book that is an inspirational source.

Many people in the world have run out of inspirational options. It is unwise to seek inspiration from an alcoholic beverage or other unhealthy vices. COVID-19 is still prevalent and present, no matter how much an individual chooses to drink or smoke one's sorrows away.

We are all in a tug of war within our minds due to this pandemic. If one does not strive to receive internal inspiration from within, then there is a chance that the individual will be living and breathing but not really fully present. This is not the way that one should aspire to experience life, though we are all in the midst of an invisible global war over our overall wellness and health.

I am fully aware that COVID-19 is a disease which has caused many to feel fearful, hopeless, and not motivated to see what the future might bring. Realistically, there will be other catastrophic events which will challenge an individual's joy and inspirational outlook. One must decide if one will allow events in this life—which one does not have any control of—ruin one's hope for the world to come, or decide to live inspired by the only joy that one can receive: and that is a relationship with the heavenly Father and Savior.

A meaningful life in this era of COVID-19 is the goal that many living during these times must aspire to. The one thing that I have learned from this viral outbreak is life, through difficult circumstances, can become inspirational. As a nation, it will be inspiring when a vaccine is able to help those who happen to contract the virus recover without experiencing any long-term effects from the illness.

When an individual who is infected with the COVID-19 virus is able to survive the disease at this present time, that is definitely inspiring and amazing. Right now, healthcare workers are limited by how they are able to treat someone who is stricken with the virus. I can only imagine how frustrating it is for the medical team and the patient to fight a battle with an invisible illness which has not been fully resolved.

Though we are in a life-and-death battle each day with the threat of the COVID-19 virus, there is still life that has to be lived. This virus has brought the purpose of life into the forefront. Some might not realize how much of an inspiration they truly are to those who are viewing individuals fighting a severe battle with this virus.

It takes a courageous and determined individual to persevere through the ups and downs of a viral illness. Not seeing one's family and loved ones for a significant amount of time is not for the individual who is easily ready to surrender to life's challenges and trials. Individuals who are battling the disease alone and in isolation do not understand how much of an inspiration and example they are to those who could potentially be in that same situation.

There are some who cannot encounter challenges in life without consulting someone. An individual who is placed in the ICU in a serious battle with the COVID-19 virus may not be fortunate enough to have support physically from those who one cherishes the most. In some severe cases of COVID-19, I have seen some infected with the disease hooked onto a ventilator.

Most individuals in that state cannot talk. Imagine and empathize with how an individual on the brink of death must feel. He or she is alone with their thoughts and with a machine that is responsible for that individual's life at that moment.

If an individual whose life was relegated to a machine can survive that ordeal, then there is not any other person who that individual cannot essentially inspire. Coming from the midst of the grave to making a full recovery from a life-threatening virus might seem as though it was coming from a movie screen. There have been individuals who have been in that same scenario who have unknowingly inspired the medical team caring for them with their relentless will.

The meaning of life is fulfilled when challenges are overcome and defeated. It is always inspiring to see an individual fight through improbable odds. Trials and challenges in one's life can sometimes inspire others without the individual who inspires desiring to take full credit.

Peace in this worldwide epidemic has become difficult to obtain. Since the onset of this widespread infectious disease pandemic, a life of peace has been replaced with ambulance sirens and death. The days of peace and serenity might seem to some that it has faded away.

Do you think that we will ever experience life without conflict? I can honestly say that those who have lived their lives having faith in the Creator and the Blessed Savior will one day enjoy everlasting peace and tranquility. COVID-19 has been the antithesis of inspiration and peace. Each day, our quest for peace is disturbed by another individual succumbing to the COVID-19 virus.

It does not require an individual with an enormous amount of wisdom to know that the times in which we live are far from being peaceful. Before the onset of this pandemic, our world has been headed for destruction. Now I consider myself an optimistic individual, but realistically, our society is on the brink of utter ruin.

For some, it took a global pandemic to realize how the world is on a collision course to chaos. Though I have stated the obvious direction of our world and society, inwardly we can develop peace and joy as well as inspiration, although the outside world is continuously perishing. As mortal beings, we have to look beyond the outbreak of the COVID-19 virus.

Instead of worrying about if you will become infected with the virus, strive to seek a life of peace for inspiration. One must have the inner peace which surpasses all the potential outside forces that could affect an individual's internal mindset. When one can acquire the peace that is not predicated on the absence of chaos and difficulty, that individual will experience a form of peace and inspiration which the world itself cannot provide.

You might be asking yourself, "How can I develop genuine peace and inspiration when the world is experiencing perilous trials and negative events?" As I stated previously, one cannot have the peace, inspiration, and courage it requires to face life's challenges without a relationship with the Messiah. Human wisdom cannot compare to divine heavenly wisdom and grace. We have to go beyond our finite capabilities to understand or comprehend the mind of Christ.

Only through a relationship with the Savior can one have a life of peace and inspiration when a deadly pandemic is dominating the world. This concept of inspiration and peace is foreign to those influenced by worldly cares. I am not suggesting that we treat the COVID-19 virus just like any other disease or pestilence, because it is not ordinary but rare.

Also, COVID-19 has exploded into a worldly concern in only a few short months. The state of our world affairs is extremely important. When I say that one can still enjoy peace, joy, and inspiration, I am simply saying that those things can be experienced when it is already assembled in one's mind.

I liken an individual experiencing peace and inspiration to an individual having fun on a rainy day. Just because the weather outside is unfavorable does not mean that the individual within should be sad. In regard to COVID-19, we can still have peace and inspiration internally, although the world is in turmoil, in spite of it.

Persevering through this pandemic is deserving of one becoming inspired. If one can overcome the chaotic COVID-19 virus, that individual has a blueprint for endurance and hope. We all are walking and talking inspirations each time we are blessed to have another day on this earth.

Although our country is divided on many issues, the one thing that we all have in common is trying to avoid becoming plagued with the virus. Sometimes difficult times can bring individuals who are bitter enemies together. I am inspired when two individuals overlook their differences for the greater good.

Every individual living during these difficult and unprecedented times needs to become encouraged. It might seem as though life is a challenge which one cannot overcome, but I believe that these times of difficulty will serve as inspiration and motivation when an individual is able to reflect. Making it through the year of the COVID-19 pandemic is definitely inspiring.

One thing that this viral outbreak has taught me is some will experience a mindset of self-pity, while others will step up to the plate and rise to the occasion. An individual who views the COVID-19 virus as a necessary trial of life is the one who will refuse to surrender to misfortune. The never-say-die attitude of some during this challenging time is the type of attitude in which others become inspired and influenced.

There are some who have lost the battle with COVID-19 who still fought the disease until the bitter end. Some individuals are inspiring to others while facing an inevitable death. One who does not yield to pity and blame when on the brink of perishing are the individuals who are examples of those displaying a valiant effort in spite of the challenging circumstances.

Though the United States has experienced great turmoil in recent years, it is still a country which consists of individuals who persevered through trials. COVID-19 might have altered the lives of many, but it has not influenced some to surrender. Individuals with that kind of mindset will inspire many others to strive for victory in the battle over one's mental and physical health.

We all love stories of overcoming enormous odds through perseverance. Because someone has the ability to endure, each experience with a trial is unique to each individual. In other words, your trial experience might not be as challenging to you than the other individual experiencing the same type of trial and vice versa.

The COVID-19 virus may not have affected some individual's health, but it might have resulted in layoffs and unemployment. It is extremely difficult to draw inspiration when an individual and their family are experiencing the effects of this virus in that way. Becoming affected by the disease in any sort of negative way leaves many without any other choice but to endure and persevere. Others will take notice and become inspired by one's persistence.

Being inspired by winning the war over the COVID-19 virus is the goal in which every individual who has contracted the pestilence should aspire to experience. Some who are in the news media do not always emphasize how some have overcome the viral ordeal. I am cognizant of the fact that there are still too many individuals who are perishing as a result of this infectious outbreak.

Because the virus is so widespread, many are focusing on the mounting death toll instead of the overall survival rate. Realistically, some are not inspired by survivors of the disease due to the sensationalized coverage on the pandemic. It is difficult to become inspired by surviving the disease when death is so widespread and, in many cases, unavoidable.

What can we do when we are faced with the challenge of the COVID-19 virus? I believe the best thing that one can do is rely upon love from friends and loved ones to inspire and influence one to fight and to never give up. This mindset commences when the individual has support from others, as well as experience with other challenging situations and circumstances in one's life. Life's challenges, which we all inevitably experience, is either combated by having a mentality of victory or the agony of defeat.

An individual who is inspired by becoming victorious over whatever difficulties that might come one's way can face the challenge of contracting the COVID-19 virus. COVID-19 is a physical and mental nightmare for some. I am not saying that just because one is inspired to overcome the illness that it will automatically mean the disease is easy to combat.

As a society, we have succumbed to being uninspired. The hearts and minds of many living during these times are filled with gloom and negativity. Every individual must realize how the thoughts and mind of an individual is crucial in life's battles.

One must not allow the negative coverage of the COVID-19 virus to influence one not to strive to overcome it. Those who have thought in their minds that they cannot defeat the disease upon contracting it have already conceded to the disease. An individual with that particular mindset is not at all inspired to fight the virus with every fiber of one's being.

I wholeheartedly believe in mental visioning for an individual's life. Having a positive image of victory over situations which might seem unbearable inspires me to continue to fight and persevere in the midst of difficult challenges. Are you motivated and inspired to continue the day-to-day struggle over staying well and healthy due to the COVID-19 virus? I understand how the talk of remaining healthy could become overwhelming and troublesome.

In regard to being inspired, one can always acquire it in times of adversity and misfortune. COVID-19 can result in some losing their will to become inspired. My suggestion to the individual who feels that way is to remember how you were able to overcome other trials. Life in this world will always consist of challenges and mishaps, but only you can obtain inspiration from situations and circumstances experienced as a result of COVID-19, which has forced some to continue to persevere with inspiration and hope.

CHAPTER 10

Maintain a Positive Perspective

You might be thinking to yourself, *How can I have a positive perspective of life when the world is suffering through a deadly pandemic?* I would say that one must go back to the basics in life. Instead of sweating the small things, appreciate the fact that you have a chance to become a better person tomorrow than the person you were the day before. Some are oblivious of how blessed they truly are.

Due to the devastation and destruction of the COVID-19 virus, it is a new day for our country, the United States. Yes, we are still a democracy, but the nation can longer boast about its economic success and stability. Many of the citizens of America are in dire need.

I never thought that I would see the day when lines for the bare essentials, such as food, would be stretched beyond what the eye can see. A plethora of families who have enjoyed immense opulence are now forced to be among the less fortunate and common folk in regard to receiving everyday products. COVID-19 is a disease that has definitely changed the economic and financial landscape of our nation.

An individual living in this country in the era of COVID-19 has to be concerned about a plethora of things all at once. For instance, one must try to become cautious of contracting the virus, number one. If one is fortunate enough to be employed and the individual is not working from home, I can only imagine the continuous feeling of anxiety when someone has to be around others who may or may not be a carrier of the virus.

Also, the individual living during these times must do one's best to remain healthy. Many are skeptical about going to clinics and hospitals due to overcrowding. One might have an illness that is not the COVID-19 virus, but because the medical staff are overwhelmed and bombarded with patient after patient, an individual might not be a priority for the overworked staff or the individual seeking medical attention could ultimately become ill or be mistaken as a COVID-19 patient.

Hopefully you are fortunate enough to not experience those kinds of issues. If you have gone through any of the problems I just discussed, try to always find the positive perspective from that particular situation. This virus could ultimately help an individual learn the value of life.

Those who value life will not have a pessimistic outlook. Individuals who have an optimistic perspective in regard to issues and problems will typically have that same mindset when these things inevitably arise. In other words, these particular individuals view the glass as half-full instead of half-empty.

What type of individual are you during this pandemic? Are you an individual who has hope that pestilences in the world will eventually become a nonissue in the coming future? Remember, from a spiritual perspective, there is another world which some will be able to fortunately experience. If you are still one to maintain a glimmer of hope in the resolving of this virus, then your perspective is positive.

Family, friends, and loved ones are vital during this pandemic. It is imperative that one has at least one family member or friend who checks on them. Our society has eventually turned into a virtual way of communicating in just about every aspect of life, which includes family, friends, and one's job for some.

Though it is suggested by experts that we physically distance ourselves from all individuals who do not live in the same household, it does not mean that we cannot talk to our friends or family members over the phone or FaceTime. There are some who complain about being limited to technological devices in order to see or converse with those who we hold dear. A positive way of viewing that scenario is realizing that this method of communicating is practical and safe.

In addition, one can appreciate friends and family more when one is physically limited in face-to-face interaction. Please do not mistake me. Personally, I favor the old way of interacting with others who we know. Due to this widespread epidemic, every individual has to rely upon what is suggested by infectious disease experts in order to remain healthy and alive.

I can recall an old saying which states, "Absence makes the heart grow fonder." This saying, I can imagine, has been in the hearts and minds of many living during these times. Grandparents and grandchildren are examples of people who have been significantly affected by this pandemic.

Some grandparents and grandchildren have seen one another in person by physically distancing themselves. I have seen some grandchildren talk to their grandparents through a glass window which served as a barrier between them. From a positive perspective, although children may not be able to physically hug their grandparents, due to the potential of an elderly individual's health becoming compromised and affected by COVID-19, at least they (the grandchildren) were able to physically see their grandparents face-to-face and in person.

Every individual residing in this era of the COVID-19 virus must strive to discover a positive perspective in spite of these negative circumstances. I believe that one can find some form of optimism. The one thing that all individuals can gain from a positive perspective is gratitude for one's life and health.

Individuals who have experienced a bout with the COVID-19 virus should also have that same perspective and mindset. It is an accomplishment for any individual to overcome a viral disease which, as of now, seems uncontrollable. This is why many who have battled COVID-19 are thankful to experience another day.

When someone can be on the brink of death and survive, that individual will have a new perspective and viewpoint on overcoming situations which might have seemed difficult and unlikely to be overcome. He or she cannot help but to have a positive way of viewing trials. I am aware that maintaining a positive perspective on life can become challenging, but it can be acquired when an individual can develop joy and contentment.

If you are alive and well at this very moment, then you are capable of having a positive outlook. COVID-19—the disease itself should not dictate whether an individual remains joyful or optimistic. As a nation, we have to somehow continue to do all that we can in this life-and-death battle.

The COVID-19 virus has affected the mental health and psyche of many. It is easy to have a positive mindset when life is going well. Many are remaining hopeful that this pandemic will soon pass or not be as detrimental to our society.

COVID-19 has taught me a valuable lesson on life. The lesson that was revealed to me in the months of struggle over sustaining relatively decent health is that it is imperative that every individual seek their purpose in life with optimism and faith. Once an individual can understand their life's purpose, it will become easier to maintain a positive perspective.

Also, I have learned how life is never promised or guaranteed. One could be healthy and vibrant one day, and on the following day, either lose one's health or perish from the virus. No one can say with assurance how one will be one, two, or even five years from now.

We all must have our priorities in order. Life is not about the accumulation of riches and possessions. I hope that the COVID-19 virus has taught that lesson to the masses.

Due to the economic decline of the United States, there is less pressure to keep up appearances. Those who were wealthy before the onset of COVID-19 have an unfamiliar set of circumstances. Many who have lost fortunes due to this worldwide epidemic must rely upon one's mental mindset and perspective instead of vast riches.

Another lesson in which many of the citizens of the United States have also learned due to the negative economic influence of COVID-19 is that riches in life is fleeting, and they do not last forever. There are a plethora of individuals whose whole identity is predicated on the appearance of being wealthy. What some whose only joy comes from money and possessions fail to realize, is that a clear and healthy mind with a positive perspective will always outlast an abundant lifestyle.

I am hopeful that this viral outbreak has influenced many to appreciate what truly matters in life. The society in which we live has stressed the myth that an individual's life is incomplete without money and power. In the grand scheme of things, one's positive mindset will result in peace and contentment despite the onset of a global, destructive, and chaotic pandemic.

You can obtain a positive perspective although life as we know has gone downward. I do not profess to know that it will be easy to continue to have this perspective each day that this pandemic is progressively worsening, but one does have a choice on whether or not they will strive to discover the silver lining in a negative circumstance. Focusing on the Creator and the daily activities that you enjoy could positively affect your perspective in a positive way. We need to continue to maintain our mental health in order to sustain a positive outlook.

Creativity in these times can prove beneficial. Some have been forced to become creative in their life due to the loss of employment. One might not be cognizant about how creativity will influence one's mood and mental stability.

For myself, I enjoy writing and creating manuscripts from scratch. Frankly, I do not know if I could have had a positive perspective in the midst of this viral outbreak if I did not have an outlet like writing to express myself. Creating and writing works for me, but some have other ways of releasing their feelings while in a pandemic.

A positive way of viewing one's circumstances as a result of the virus is that this is the time to establish one's creative ambitions. There are some dreams which one might have set aside pre-pandemic. When an individual discovers their creative talent, he or she will have a positive perspective on one's ability to develop a new project.

Some individuals have the God-given ability to create art. Before the pandemic, an individual who was blessed with that particular talent would not entertain the thought of pursuing a dream of becoming an artist. Now one might have the time to pursue a career in art due to their belief and positive perception of oneself.

This virus has ultimately influenced many to make lemonade out of lemons. A mentality of creating something is only derived from a positive mindset and outlook. Exercising one's creativity during these unprecedented and difficult times gives the individual a sense of purpose and hope.

We must always strive to have a positive perspective of life; although, the virus is not influencing one to have that type of perspective. Suppose you do not have a positive outlook because you are worried and concerned about the state of our world and nation. I would suggest that you do your best to develop your gratitude in regard to having life and being able to live through a potentially deadly and dangerous disease epidemic.

COVID-19 has challenged many in our world and society to search the individual within. I am certain that many are reflecting and also self-examining themselves. If you are doing those things, know that it is imperative to discover more positive attributes of oneself than negative ones.

Individuals living during this era of the COVID-19 virus have to basically reprogram themselves. Having ambitions of material success should not be one's goal in these times, because everything is becoming increasingly scarce and difficult to come by. What do you have left when all your material wealth is gone? The only thing left is who you are at the core.

When the layers of an individual are peeled back, that person must decide how they will proceed. The COVID-19 virus has some considering moving forward in life in spite of ongoing chaos. Moving forward in this era of the global pandemic can only result from the development of a positive self-examination.

Before COVID-19 became rampant in our country, there was a plethora of pollution in many of our American cities. The quality of air was poor due to the busyness of industries, such as the airlines which produced pollution from air travel. Also, the most obvious threat of poor air quality from many of our metropolises in the United States is the pollution cars driving in these cities produced.

Bumper-to-bumper traffic along with car exhaustion are recipes for a pollution disaster. When many cities initially suspended most business operations, there was less traffic on the road. Something positive resulted from less cars being on the highways and busy interstates.

The positive circumstance that having less car traffic on the road resulted in was better air quality. I personally viewed a side-by-side comparison between the air in Los Angeles, California, before the onset of COVID-19 and after, and the air was not filled with smog when the city had a decrease in car activity. You might be wondering why I am discussing pollution and air quality.

I am briefly discussing these issues because it is an example of something positive that has resulted from the COVID-19 virus. As individuals living in difficulty, we have to discover something beneficial from this viral pandemic. If you are the type of individual who relishes finding optimism in a negative situation, then you are an individual with a positive perspective.

An individual who has a relatively high level of optimism could be challenged by all the negative energy from others in our society which stems from the threat of COVID-19 in every aspect of life. One must come to the realization that the COVID-19 virus will weigh heavily on the individual who cannot take something negative and turn it into something positive. It is as though this virus has become an infectious cancer of gloom and negativity.

We all know that some cancers spread throughout the whole entire body. This form of the disease is the most dangerous and detrimental to not only an individual's physical health but mentally; it can become quite draining and deflating when the individual does not put a positive spin on it. COVID-19 also has an effect on an individual that is similar to various types of cancer.

Mental anguish, which is not dealt with as a result of the COVID-19 virus, could become a mental cancer to one's emotions. Once an individual's feelings and emotions spirals negatively, it can become difficult to regain a positive outlook. Hence, a negative psychological take over.

One might not be mindful of the importance of a positive mental mindset in spite of a negative occurrence or event, but it ultimately helps weaken the impact. Strive to identify when you are tempted to allow this virus to consume your thoughts. Replace that temptation for negativity with thoughts of victory and hope.

Are you aware of who you are mentally? Sure, one might think they know the type of individual who one aspires to become, but the COVID-19 virus has revealed the person you are presently. No one will truly know the individual who one truly is until one is forced to encounter adversity. This virus can either make an individual have a positive mental imagery of oneself, or a pessimistic imagery and mindset of self.

Basically, what I am saying is that an individual's whole mental perception is formulated when the individual experiences and conquers life's challenges. The COVID-19 virus is a challenge and trial which requires one to adapt psychologically to the new reality in our society. There is a possibility that in the best-case scenario, our nation can function properly again.

In order for that to occur, the majority of individuals in our country will need to refer to other countries that have gotten the COVID-19 virus under control. South Korea was among the first countries to experience the outbreak of this viral pandemic. They went through a difficult period in their battle with COVID-19, but ultimately prevailed on the victorious side in the fight against it.

As a nation, the United States can gain a positive perspective of hope on the taming of the COVID-19 virus from the example from a foreign land. The United States is just as capable as any other country in limiting the spread of COVID-19. This is one reason why I have maintained hope and optimism that our nation can as a whole become a country which could successfully excel in overcoming this infectious viral threat.

It will require a shift in the attitudes of many of the citizens of America. Many who reside in this country are stubborn and do not like to be told what to do or how to behave. I believe that if citizens of this country view precautions and guidelines in diminishing the spread of COVID-19 from a positive perspective, the disease could eventually subside and have no existing effects.

Also, self-control and discipline are key factors in combating this epidemic. One has to demonstrate the restraint and the ability to do what leading experts on infectious diseases, such as COVID-19, are telling one to do. We all have the capability of following and taking heed to instructions.

Some are unaware of how vital following instructions are in the COVID-19 battle. Citizens of countries that have been able to overcome this pandemic had the discipline of quarantining and not going out in public unless it was absolutely necessary. The difference between this country and other countries is perspective and perception.

If one perceives the limit on public outings as a negative problem, then one's perspective will be the antithesis of something positive. As a country and nation, we must be receptive to the sage advice of what disease experts are suggesting that every individual in this nation must do in order to defeat the spread of the virus. We must adapt a positive perspective when it comes to the virus by viewing the limitations, protocols, and guidelines as necessary instead of harmful.

Negative and catastrophic events like the COVID-19 virus are oftentimes a chance for one to grow and mature spiritually and psychologically. It might seem as though when an individual is in the midst of an unfavorable situation, it will not eventually end. In the aftermath of a trial, an individual has one's own perspective of the misfortune left to assess.

I beg to differ with those who cannot find the positive lesson from something that has resulted in hurt and pain. The COVID-19 virus is an illness that has destroyed and affected many families nationwide, as well as all around the world. No one can bring back the victims who have succumbed to the virus, but from a positive perspective in regard to an individual perishing from a severe bout with COVID-19, at least the individual does not have to suffer in excruciating pain and discomfort.

For individuals who have survived the COVID-19 battle, hopefully one will be able to help other victims of the disease cope with the lingering physical and psychological effects which can stem from being infected with the virus. In my opinion, an individual who has experienced a debilitating illness, such as the COVID-19 virus, is able to share a unique perspective to others encountering the same experience. Someone who has battled the disease and survived it will offer hope and confidence to another individual who might have a negative perspective in regard to the illness.

When an individual feels that another individual can relate and have empathy, he or she will most likely thrive. Those who have support from others who have contracted and defeated the virus will have a positive perspective. An optimistic perspective can help an individual in the midst of a life-and-death battle with the COVID-19 virus to have the peace and strength to accept whatever circumstances the battle and struggle will ultimately result in.

If someone who has contracted the virus, overcomes the illness and is experiencing the physical effects from it, my hope is that they do not become sad and frustrated. There is always a reason and a purpose for everything that happens in life, whether good or bad. Someone with a positive perspective on life will come to that realization.

We all must face some type of challenge in life. Some may not have experienced any semblance of a trial until COVID-19 became an issue. Trials and negative occurrences such as the COVID-19 virus typically do not affect the masses in the way that it essentially did.

Occurrences that affect millions worldwide are usually a result of a military war. This virus is an invisible enemy, which can only begin and end with a positive attitude. In the United States, it is imperative that its citizens learn how to become receptive to what is suggested for their own good.

Cooperation and patience are needed in order to decrease the high death toll rates of this pandemic in this country. You might not be cognizant of how a positive attitude toward what is needed in the prevention of COVID-19 can go a long way. The battle with this infectious disease is won with optimism and patience.

Problems and issues in life are sure ways to advance in growth, patience, and maturity. The COVID-19 virus, though it is not a positive occurrence, is essentially a test. There are some tests in life which do not require drastic lifestyle changes.

For decades, our democracy has become complacent. In 1918, when the Spanish Flu also affected millions worldwide, the United

States was not viewed back then, as a legitimate Super Power. This is because the nation was in the midst of World War I.

Fast-forward to the years after World War II and the Vietnam War, this nation has enjoyed many decades of economic and financial stability. Because of the nation's obsession with wealth and power, moral values and attitudes have become less of a priority. Instead of valuing people, this country has collectively, as a whole, valued wealth, abundance, and status over the concern for one's neighbor.

One must realistically admit that many in our country have the wrong perspective. It is wrong, as well as a negative quality, to be so ambitious for money and wealth that one will compromise and sacrifice one's family and love in order to gain financial success. An individual with that mindset and perspective is never satisfied.

Everything in our world and life changed in the year of 2020. COVID-19 became the great neutralizer in economic success for millions, particularly in America. This pandemic has affected the priorities and life perspectives of many.

When the United States became affected economically by COVID-19, it forced many of the citizens who worshipped wealth to develop another perspective in regard to people and money. Because millions of Americans have lost their ability to acquire great abundance, it has influenced many to value life and people instead of riches and glory. Some might not see the transition of our country being financially driven to becoming a country that is people oriented. There are some who do not realize that this is a positive thing, but it is.

Now that we are in a position of economic distress as a country, some individuals will commence to value life itself as opposed to material things which will soon not have any value in the world to come. The COVID-19 virus is the sole reason why America is starting to prioritize health instead of wealth.

Though it is never a welcomed sight to see most Americans struggle with the basic essentials as a result of the COVID-19 virus, choosing to value the lives of others is definitely a positive result from this viral pestilence. Due to the mass majority of citizens of the United States having to adapt to a new way of living, a positive aspect of this new normal in life is the ability of others to relate and empathize with others. Empathy is a trait that many have lacked in this country and also elsewhere.

It is unfortunate that a global pandemic has altered the lives of millions, but it has also allowed others to value life. There is more life to gain if the mystery of the virus can be solved. Never relinquish your optimistic vision that the COVID-19 virus will one day become a nonfactor.

Maintaining a positive perspective in the era of the COVID-19 virus is vital. One has to be careful not to allow oneself to sink into a pessimistic mindset due to what is occurring nationwide, as well as all over the world. In my opinion, this virus has influenced some to appreciate the value of life.

As a nation, we must strive to acquire optimism in the midst of this COVID-19 storm. An individual who has a positive attitude and mindset is not oblivious of all the destruction and turmoil that a storm produces, but he or she anticipates overcoming it. The COVID-19 virus is a storm we as a society do not have any other choice but to face and endure.

If you can battle and overcome COVID-19 with limited resources to combat it, then you are extremely fortunate and in rare company. There are many who have decided to either deny the severity of COVID-19, or downplay the potential effect that the virus could have on one's life. Having an authentic positive perspective in regard to the COVID-19 virus will only come into fruition when an individual can envision the time that the destruction of the disease will subside.

I am aware that currently the COVID-19 virus is having its way with destroying and taking away innocent lives. No one deserves to lose their life to a virus that usually results in an infected individual dying alone in severe cases. Although this pandemic is responsible for invoking fear and anxiety, there is hope that it will one day become a disease which can be tamed and controlled.

I believe that there is always something positive which can result from a challenging situation. Maybe the onset of this virus could cause estranged families to interact with one another again. Another way of positively viewing the result of this destructive virus is how it has influenced some to examine their own careless behavior.

We cannot control what will happen to us in life in many instances, but we can decide internally how we will respond and view those trials that occur in life. One must strive to avoid a negative attitude due to this virus. An overall mindset of hope and courage to live life in the most positive and optimistic way in which one knows how is all that an individual living in the COVID-19 era can do mentally.

This is the perfect time to work on the individual inside of you. The COVID-19 virus has inadvertently caused some to psychologically question the person who they really are internally. One should consider developing and building one's mental outlook in the midst of this horrendous pandemic and unprecedented time in our human existence.

Life's battles are usually overcome with the right perspective. If you have an optimistic perspective, regardless of this devastating epidemic, I am confident that this perspective can become a reason for conquering and overcoming a negative situation and event. COVID-19 is a battle and storm in which all are affected. As a society, a positive perspective is crucial in weathering this unprecedented and unforeseen storm.

Throughout this book, I have tried to be realistic and also encourage those having difficulty with the current state in our world and society, as a result of the COVID-19 virus, to have a positive mindset in spite of it. We must come to the realization that our lives are vastly different than the way it was previously. Some do not like what our society has become due to this epidemic.

Change means a fresh start. The COVID-19 virus has literally been responsible for many starting their lives over. Please do not mistake me: I understand that this virus has caused millions in this country, as well as worldwide, to be displaced from their families and homes. A plethora of individuals are having difficulty in trying to maintain the same lifestyle they had pre-pandemic.

My hope and prayer for those experiencing difficulties due to this virus is that the individuals who are affected by this global pandemic physically, psychologically, and financially do not give up on themselves and life. This is a challenge in our world's history unlike any other challenge experienced by most nations simultaneously. In the United States alone, the COVID-19 virus is escalating into uncharted territory in regard to the number of daily deaths.

Resiliency, optimism, and perseverance are needed in this worldwide and societal battle with this invisible enemy. One must not be overwhelmed mentally by fear of contracting the disease. If you do all that is required of you in avoiding contracting the virus, you can easily have mental assurance.

Our psychological and mental mindset are key components in battling the COVID-19 illness while living in the era of this epidemic. Individuals battling the virus in ICUs around the world are in great physical pain and stress. It is difficult to maintain and sustain an optimistic attitude while facing a life-and-death struggle.

Optimism is imperative during this pandemic because it is synonymous with hope. We must have hope that this trial will one day pass. Now no one knows whether or not the vaccines that were developed will significantly turn the tide in a positive direction when it comes to the decreasing of the COVID-19 virus.

The world in which we live, as a whole, does not always acknowledge hope and optimism when difficulties and misfortune are prevalent. As a society, we tend to focus on the negative issues instead. COVID-19 has many in our world complaining and being pessimistic about what this pestilence is doing to millions.

COVID-19 should not stop one from having optimism and enjoying life. What I mean by enjoying life is being content with whatever situation or circumstance you are currently in. Hope and optimism commences from within, and by now, one should realize that external factors in life are not always sustainable and everlasting when it comes to one's happiness. So in light of this chaotic disturbance called COVID-19, which has suddenly and mysteriously burst upon the scene, one should try to always maintain some form of optimism and joy in spite of the challenging circumstances in this chaotic-filled world.

ABOUT THE AUTHOR

Romain U. DuFour III is a graduate of the University of Houston-Downtown with a bachelor's degree in psychology. The author desires to spread a positive message to all who are serious and dedicated readers.